THE ACCO
GUID
PRAC
PROMOTION

THE ACCOUNTANT'S GUIDE TO PRACTICE PROMOTION

Patrick Forsyth

Marketing Improvements Limited

Published in Association with
The Institute of Chartered Accountants
in England and Wales

KOGAN
PAGE

For Drummond, an early and successful convert

First published in 1988 by
Kogan Page Ltd,
120 Pentonville Rd, London N1 9JN

Printed and bound in Great Britain by
Biddles Ltd, Guildford, Surrey.

British Library Cataloguing in Publication Data
Forsyth, Patrick
    The accountant's guide to practice promotion
    1. Marketing — For accountancy
    I. Title
    658.8′ 024657

    ISBN 1-85091-629-2

Contents

Preface

Not so very long ago the idea of a book on the marketing of accountancy services would have been viewed with a mixture of amazement and horror. The profession enjoyed increasing prosperity in what most outsiders regarded as a highly protected environment. Profit growth was assured as audit volumes increased with the growth of the market; future planning was easy because so many of the inputs could be taken as fixed.

Today, much of that certainty has disappeared. Two factors, inextricably linked, have in many countries changed the face of the accountants' world for ever. First, the ethical restrictions which prohibited most forms of promotional activity have been progressively relaxed. Secondly, the certainty of work 'walking through the door' almost as and when required has gone – accountancy is now as competitive as most other business fields and more so than many.

The competitive pressures are there for all to see, and show themselves in three main areas. First 'professional' competition, (ie that from other practising firms) especially the large firms taking different attitudes to their own growth. Secondly, competition from outside the practising profession, for example the work being done by banks, management consultants and others. Thirdly, client pressure, a much greater demand for value for money reflected in many ways even to the extent of 'shopping around' for the audit. And no matter how much repeat business is done, the proportion of total fees that needs to be sought out is growing and converting prospects, referrals and enquiries – even new projects with existing clients – is becoming less certain and demands a more professional approach.

These trends continue. As the market for professional accountancy services grows, who gets that growth, and indeed who books any new business is influenced in turn by the continuing debate on professional ethics, which has to some degree slowed progress towards a true marketing approach in the UK and elsewhere.

But a lot has been done over the past few years, certainly by some. Tentatively at first, accountants have dipped their toes in the marketing stream. At first marketing was equated with advertising. So advertising was tried. Soon it was realized that there were other possibilities. Public Relations and other promotional activity. More recently, direct mail has been included among permitted techniques. And more accountants have been designated 'Marketing Partner', set promotional budgets, and are even regarded as having a sales role.

Whether this whole process is regarded as revolution or evolution, it has certainly changed the face of accountancy. Already, looking back, surrounded by a plethora of marketing activity, the days when none of this was necessary seem a long time ago. Originally there was a strong feeling within the profession that what would result from all these changes was simply 'the situation as was, plus some advertising'. In fact everything has changed. Attitudes and practices with regard to services, fees, practice organization, the promotional mix, training and even recruitment of staff have all been affected. Muted talk of 'practice development' has given way to a situation where marketing has become the watchword of many.

But does marketing really apply to *professional* services?

If a professional firm is to survive and prosper, then patently it must organize its activities in such a way that the fees and revenues it can earn from the supply of its services exceed the costs of those services. Indeed in many cases it must do more – it must produce sufficient growth both of profit and range of interesting work so that it can provide the satisfactions necessary to attract and keep the level of first-class staff to supply the partners of tomorrow, to provide a future for the firm as a whole. Therefore, the firm must be constantly aware of the need to offer services to clients which fulfil not only statutory but also commercial needs; and to fulfil these needs better than competition at cost-effective fee levels.

To do this the needs of the client and the market must be defined, the appropriate services for today (and tomorrow) must be developed; the fee levels which are both competitive and profitable must be set; the services available must be communicated to existing and prospective clients so that they are persuaded to buy them. Thus the main marketing tactics, research, product/service development, pricing and promotion all have a part to play in the successful firm. (This is true, not only of accountants but is in many ways similar for other professional services; the review of these elements that make up this book will therefore be relevant and useful to those in such allied area as consultancy, and to those such as solicitors, surveyors, architects and others facing essentially the same situation.)

Of course, some marketing tactics appropriate to other industries will be neither applicable nor effective. In-store merchandizing or door-to-door selling are of little use to the profession. However, no commercial company can usefully employ all the marketing and promotional tactics. It is the company's or firm's decision as to which tactics are most appropriate or cost-effective. However, it is hard to identify any examples of a company where marketing has no application at all.

Marketing focuses the drive for growth and profit, it stimulates the whole process of client satisfaction which is the motivation for so many accountants. Its adoption represents a major opportunity for the profession, yet, as a wise man once said 'the trouble with opportunities is that they are often disguised as hard work'.

With this in mind, this book sets out the key elements of marketing as it applies to accountancy. It explains what marketing is, it shows what techniques it includes and how they can be used, and it provides guidelines from which any practice, large or small, can begin to implement marketing as it is right for them.

Marketing is as much an art as a science. It needs to be applied both creatively and systematically. The process is not easy and represents a challenge to many in the profession. There is no one right way. The adoption of marketing to accountancy has been and remains an area of continuing change. So while the ideas reviewed here represent the best current practice as this book goes to press, they are unlikely to be the final word. Accountancy exists in dynamic and exciting times.

Patrick Forsyth
Marketing Improvements Limited
Ulster House
17 Ulster Terrace
Outer Circle, Regents Park
London NW1 4PS

Acknowledgements

Much of the material in this book first appeared in print as a number of publications (listed below*) put out by the Institute of Chartered Accountants of England and Wales. Thanks are thus due to that body for giving their blessing to publication in this form; and to Phil Shohet, Nick Tarrant and John Pepper for whose editorial advice I was grateful as those earlier publications were prepared.

Thanks are also due to my colleagues at Marketing Improvements; Ian Collins and David Senton, each of whom collaborated with me on one of the earlier publications and some of whose words therefore appear in this text.

In addition, I owe a debt of gratitude to the many delegates I have found myself addressing in the last few years at a variety of courses, seminars and conferences of accountants. Their comments and contributions on these occasions have given me an increasing insight into the world of accountancy, and ensured that the concepts and ideas expressed here have a practical slant appropriate to the marketing of an accountancy practice.

* The Marketing and Selling of Accountancy Services
  Practice Promotion and Presentation
  The Practice Promotion Kit
  Client Development
  Direct Mail

Chapter 1

Introduction

**'You can't sit on the lid of progress.
If you do, you will be blown to pieces'**

Henry Kaiser

What exactly is marketing? Well for a start too often misunderstood. Certainly, despite what some firms have done, the word marketing remains confusing and the concepts and techniques involved underused.

Therefore, while the prime intention of this book is to show how a practical plan for promoting the practice can be prepared and implemented, a few words about marketing first both to recap and set the scene seem appropriate.

In some ways it is not surprising that marketing remains a confusing word as it is used in at least three different ways. Marketing is not advertising; nor is advertising a euphemism for marketing. Marketing is:

(a) *a concept,* that of seeing the business through the eyes of the customers and ensuring profitability through providing them with value satisfaction;
(b) *a function,* the total management function that coordinates the above approach, anticipating the demands of the customer, identifying and satisfying his needs via the provision of the right products or services at the right price, time and place;
(c) *a series of techniques* which make the process possible, these include advertising plus other promotional activity, sales, and also market research, pricing and others.

All are relevant and important to accountancy. The first implies that everyone in the practice is involved, everyone needs to adopt the right attitude and many will have specific roles to play. The second implies that someone within the practice wears 'the marketing hat'. This does not mean one person is involved exclusively, but responsibility, and particularly the planning and initiation of activity must lie specifically with someone. Perhaps, by definition, that person should be a good delegator!

The third implies not only that a considerable number of

techniques, many not the traditional stock in trade of the accountant, are involved and must be understood, but also that these must be used systematically and coordinated appropriately together.

So marketing is not something that can be compartmentalized. The practice does not need a cupboard of marketing techniques to be opened only when time permits or when additional business is urgently required. It needs a marketing orientation in every aspect of the practice and everyone in it needs to be involved – continuously. The process starts with the planning stage. Every business needs a plan (as you surely tell your clients) and a key element of such a plan is the marketing plan. Chapter 2 thus looks at the planning process and comments additionally on the need for a marketing view to be taken of the services offered and the fees charged. Promotional activity, everything from what letterhead the firm has, to advertising and public relations, and how it is planned and coordinated, is the subject of Chapters 3 and 4. Next direct mail, a recent addition to permitted techniques is reviewed in detail not only because it is likely to become one of the most important but because it exemplifies the approach needed if any description of services is to be persuasive.

All these promotional elements are designed to provide the direct personal contact which, perhaps best regarded as the final link in a persuasive chain, must be sales orientated. So Chapter 6 looks at personal selling and the proposal 'selling starts when the customer says yes'. This simply means that selling must continue in parallel with executing the work, existing clients are your best prospects for the future. The whole question of managing, expanding and developing client relationships is then examined in the last chapter.

I believe this makes a logical progression and indeed what is being described is a repeating cycle, but the chapters are designed to enable the reader to dip into, or revisit, one particular topic.

Chapter 2

Marketing Planning

**'If you don't know where you are going
all roads lead there'**

The Cheshire Cat in *Alice in Wonderland*

The Marketing Plan

Any firm approaching the construction of a marketing plan must recognize that the initial stages can only be the responsibility of the partners. The importance of the strategic choices which must be made cannot be delegated. Equally, to ignore the strategic stage and simply have management develop tactical plans misunderstands the whole purpose of marketing planning. Without the frame of reference provided by marketing objectives and strategies, tactical plans will have no focus and little credibility. 'If' as a wise man said, 'you don't know where you're going, any road will take you there'.

Any business, professional or commercial, has to operate in a market for its services or products. Every market segments according to the priority of needs of the various groups of clients. These needs are dynamic, and must constantly be reassessed by the supplier. Thus the firm can make optional use of its resources of time and money in its selection of the segments of the available market on which it intends to concentrate. In allocating these resources, the firm must define the appropriate framework for communicating, providing and charging for its selected range of services, and cope with the pressures of demand, competition, legal restriction and change, and the consequent availability of staff and of capital.

If a business then wishes to be more than a victim of history or circumstance, it must plan, organize and control its activities specifically and, wherever possible, quantitatively. Precise marketing planning is the only meaningful way to define how a firm wishes to relate to and influence its business environment. Form 1 shows the stages through which the plan must pass.

The Purpose of a Formal Plan

The marketing plan has three main aims. First to be certain that all the objectives set by the firm are clearly related to specific

3

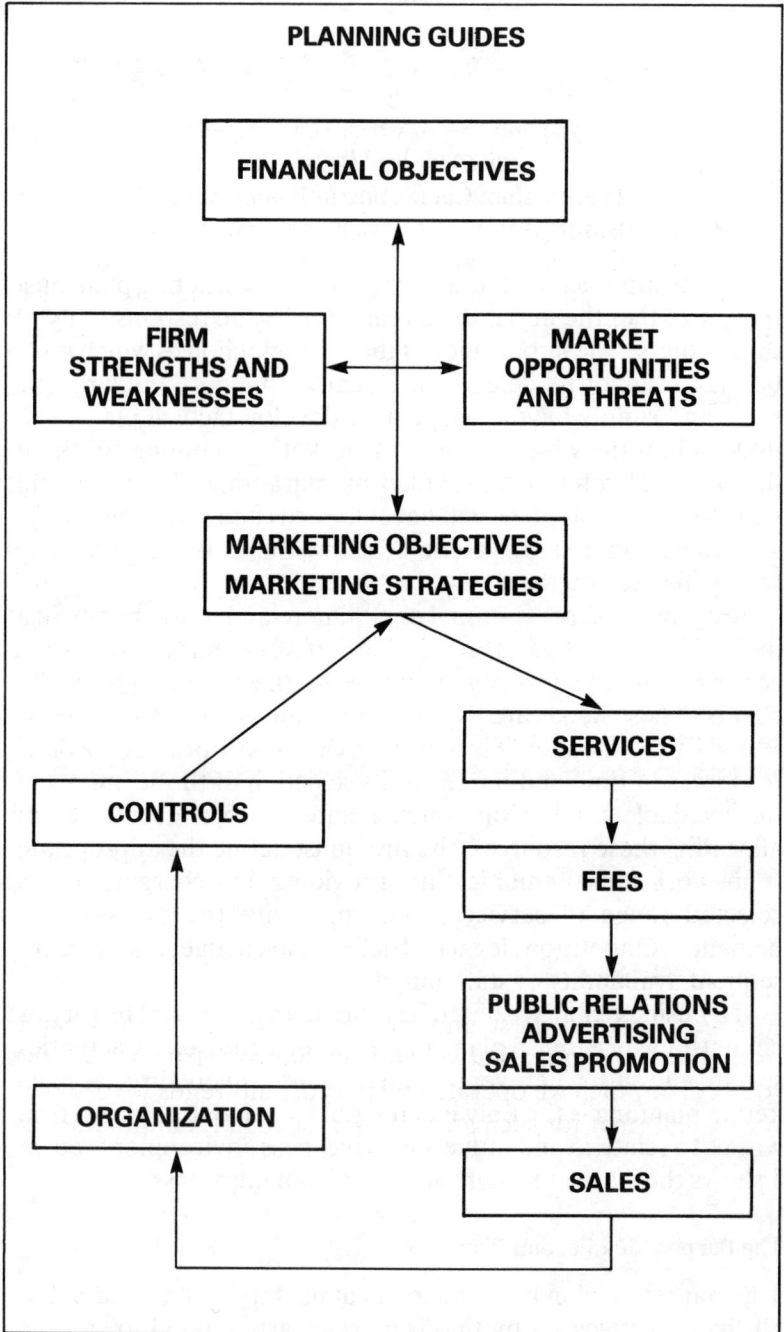

PLANNING GUIDES

```
                    ┌──────────────────────────┐
                    │   FINANCIAL OBJECTIVES   │
                    └──────────────────────────┘
                                 ↕
  ┌──────────────────┐                ┌──────────────────────┐
  │      FIRM        │                │      MARKET          │
  │ STRENGTHS AND    │ ←───────────→  │  OPPORTUNITIES       │
  │  WEAKNESSES      │                │   AND THREATS        │
  └──────────────────┘                └──────────────────────┘
                                 ↕
              ┌──────────────────────────────┐
              │   MARKETING OBJECTIVES       │
              │   MARKETING STRATEGIES       │
              └──────────────────────────────┘

                                          ┌──────────────────┐
                                          │    SERVICES      │
  ┌──────────────────┐                    └──────────────────┘
  │    CONTROLS      │                              ↓
  └──────────────────┘                    ┌──────────────────┐
                                          │      FEES        │
                                          └──────────────────┘
                                                   ↓
                                          ┌──────────────────┐
                                          │ PUBLIC RELATIONS │
  ┌──────────────────┐                    │   ADVERTISING    │
  │  ORGANIZATION    │                    │ SALES PROMOTION  │
  └──────────────────┘                    └──────────────────┘
                                                   ↓
                                          ┌──────────────────┐
                                          │     SALES        │
                                          └──────────────────┘
```

actions (and by corollary that large amounts of expensive time are not taken up by activities which have little or no effect on the achievement of objectives).

Secondly, that the individual efforts of all staff are concentrated on the actions specified by the partners or owners. In particular, all staff should be aware of the key priority actions which keep the firm in business today and tomorrow. At its simplest, this could be ensuring that every account is examined to identify additional business potential, or perhaps that invoices are submitted immediately they are due.

Thirdly, that all the activities specified in the plan can be measured, assessed and improved, as the planned year progresses.

Setting Marketing Objectives

Naturally, writing a plan presumes that partners and managers know the markets in which they operate, have clear marketing objectives, and have the power to authorize or recommend action to agreed cost levels.

All firms have financial goals expressed in budgets of fee revenue and expenditure (see Form 2). However, since sales and profits can only be made by working with clients in the markets we select, the partners' first task must be to translate the financial objectives into market objectives; they must answer the question 'what results must be achieved in the market-place to produce the financial objective we wish to see?'

Meaningful answers can only be produced by considering two interrelated analyses:
- What opportunities and threats will be present?
- What are the strengths and weaknesses of the firm?

Market Opportunities and Threats

The simplest and most unbiased way is to carry out a basic analysis of the quantitative and qualitative structure of the markets in which we operate and the current trends we can perceive. A format for such an analysis is seen in Example 1 and is recorded on Form 3.

FINANCIAL OBJECTIVES

	LAST YEAR'S ACTUAL	NEXT YEAR'S PLAN
FEES		
OTHER	_____	_____
TOTAL		
COSTS	_____	_____
PROFIT	_____	_____

EXAMPLE 1 MARKET OPPORTUNITIES AND THREATS

(1)   *How is the market structured quantitatively?*

(1.1)   *How many* people/organizations of what type are there in our market who have a need for accountancy services?
(eg, corporate/private/large/small/geographic location).

(1.2)   *What services* do they currently use?
(eg, audit/tax/consultancy).

(1.3)   *How much* of the services do they use?
(eg, annual spend).

(1.4)   *How often* do they use the services?
(eg, annually/monthly).

(1.5)   Whom do they use?

(1.6)   What services do they *not* use?
(eg, CTT advice/computer audit).

(1.7)   How do *existing* and *potential users gain access to* accountancy services?
(eg, personal recommendation/directories).

(2)   How is the market structured qualitatively?

(2.1)   *Why* do existing and potential customers buy/not buy accountancy services?
(eg, statutory requirement/unaware.

(2.2)   What do they think of the services they buy?
(eg, good value/overpriced).

(2.3)   What do they think of the firms who supply the services?
(eg, too big/too small/helpful/unhelpful).

(3)   *How is the market served competitively?*

(3.1)   Who are our *direct* competitors?
(eg, other accountancy firms).

(3.2)   Who are our *indirect* competitors?
(eg, banks/solicitors/certified accountants).

(3.3)   What are their strengths and weaknesses?
(eg, services/size/staff/image/fees/marketing skills/geographic coverage).

(4)   *What are the quantitative and qualitative trends?*
- market/segment size;
- market/segment requirements;
- market/segment structure;
- market/segment location;
- competition.

Form 3

MARKET

OPPORTUNITIES	THREATS
ACTION	ACTION

Firm's Strengths and Weaknesses

We can then assess the strengths and weaknesses of the firm against the requirements of our current and our potential markets, and compared with the abilities and services of our competitors (see Form 4). We must consider objectively and dispassionately our standing in seven key areas:

Client base;
Range of services;
Fees structure;
Promotional and selling activities;
Planning systems;
Organizational structure;
Controls and measurement procedures.

A format for such an analysis is seen in Example 2.

EXAMPLE 2   FIRM'S STRENGTHS AND WEAKNESSES

(1)   *Client base*
(1.1) What is our current client base, by size, by location, by industry?
(1.2) How does our disposition of clients (client mix) compare with the market mix?
(1.3) Are our clients in growth sectors of the market?
(1.4) How dependent are we on our largest clients?

(2)   *Range of services*
(2.1) How closely does our range of services reflect the market's needs?
(2.2) How does our range compare with competitors?
(2.3) Are the majority of our services in growth or decline?
(2.4) Is our range of services too narrow to satisfy our markets?
(2.5) Is our range too broad to allow satisfactory management of performance?

(3)   *Fee structure*
(3.1) What is the basis of our fee structure?
(3.2) Do our direct and indirect competitors structure in the same way?
(3.3) Are our fees competitive?
(3.4) Do our clients perceive fees as 'value for money'?

(4)   *Promotional and selling activities*

(4.1) With which clients/recommenders/influencers are we communicating?

(4.2) What do they know and feel about the firm?

(4.3) Are we communicating with enough of the 'right' people?

(4.4) What means of communication are we using?

(4.5) What attitudes exist in the firm towards 'selling' services?

(4.6) Is each person in contact with clients capable of selling the full range of services?

(4.7) Do they possess the necessary knowledge and skill in selling?

(5)   *Planning marketing activity*

(5.1) Do we have agreed plans for the marketing and selling activity?

(5.2) Do the plans state activities as well as objectives and budgets?

(5.3) Do we have individual as well as corporate plans?

(6)   *Organizing for marketing*

(6.1) How is the firm's marketing activity organized and coordinated?

(6.2) Are authority and responsibility for each person clearly defined?

(6.3) Are our people committed to marketing the firm and its services?

(7)   *Control and measurement of marketing*

(7.1) Have we defined *'success'* for ourselves and our staff?

(7.2) Have we established *key result areas* to measure that success?

(7.3) Do these standards examine marketing as well as professional standards?

(7.4) Do we measure performance against desired standards and take corrective action?

Clearly, this is only a skeleton and many supplementary questions may be neccessary to get specific and objective answers. What is essential is that honest examination establishes definitely the firm's standing in its markets.

Using this comparative analysis between the market and the firm, the partners and managers are in much stronger position to translate financial goals in true marketing objectives, which are achievable in the market-place but within the firm's scope.

Form 4

FIRM

STRENGTHS	WEAKNESSES
ACTION	ACTION

Without such objectives, it is impossible to focus and to place any tacticial activities in order of priority. Yet the main options available to us in marketing objectives are limited — perhaps six-fold.

- *To increase market share*
  In a static market this can be done by 'conquest' selling — winning business from other firms.

- *To expand existing markets*
  This objective will focus on selling the fullest range of our services to our exisiting clients and market. It also presumes very close cooperation bewteen audit and activities and other services.

- *To develop new services for existing markets*
  This can involve simply the revision of existing services or the introduction of radical new services, as some of the larger practices have done with computer systems.

- *To develop new markets for existing services*
  Within the UK itself this option is becoming increasingly limited, since the statutory nature of audit has already identified all major potential users. In other countries, of course, this may not be the case.

- *To develop new services in new markets*
  This is an example of true diversification. This usually carries the highest risk of all marketing objectives. Many firms do not even consider such objectives. Future pressures however for the growth necessary to keep good staff may force a reassessment.

- *To improve the profitability of existing operations*
  When growth opportunities are limited, many firms must in the short term seek higher returns from higher productivity and greater cost-effectiveness of their operations.

From the analysis of market opportunities and threats and the internal assessment of strengths and weaknesses the firm will select the marketing objective(s) which will best achieve its financial goals for the planning period (see Form 5).

Developing marketing strategies

The next stage in planning is probably both the most important and the most neglected by the majority of firms – the identification of all the potential strategies which could be followed to achieve a particular marketing objective. The two are often confused:

The objective is *a desired result* in the market-place.

The strategy is *a course of action* to achieve that result.

The purpose of the strategy is to focus effort, co-ordinate action and exploit identified strengths of the firm. By corollary, the purpose is to avoid waste of resources on peripheral and non-productive activities (see Form 5).

Clearly, different objectives will require very different strategies. Some of the main courses of action open to an accountancy firm may be as follows:

Marketing objectives	*Some possible strategy alternatives*
To increase share of the existing market	–Market segmentation and concentration of resource on selected segments –Developing service applications and range extension –Range of registered firm names for different segments.
To expand existing markets	–Increasing the frequency of client purchase –Increasing service usage (in other applications) –Opening new branches.
To develop new markets for existing services	–Expanding the range of segments currently dealt with –Overseas expansion.
To develop new services in new markets	–Diversification by purchase/take-over –Technological extension, eg financial systems into software services –Exploitation of corporate resources and skills.
To increase profitability of existing business	–Improving the total service package offered to each client account –Marketing audit and productivity analysis. –Systems selling: 'turnkey offerings' –Reduction of service range.

The selection of strategies need not be mutually exclusive. Often a combination can provide even stronger effect in marketing plans. However, the greatest danger for a firm, at the point of selecting appropriate strategies, is that it may be tempted to adopt too many courses of action. The mistake spreads management too thinly and prevents commitment of maximum effort to the prime and most important courses of action.

Marketing planning then must begin with a thorough and creative attempt to choose the most appropriate focus for the entire firm's marketing effort. The determination to concentrate simplifies the tactical marketing plans which must then follow for the range of services to be offered, the fees to be charged, and the promotional and selling actions to communicate with the chosen markets.

Form 5

+--+
| |
| **MARKETING OBJECTIVES** |
| |
| |
| |
| |
| |
| |
| |
| |
| **MARKETING STRATEGIES** |
| |
| |
| |
| |
| |
| |
| |
+--+

Tactical Marketing Planning
Establishing the range of services to be offered
The actions taken thus far have established what we wish to achieve in the market and the main lines of action most likely to achieve those objectives. Most marketing planning breaks down because these strategic aims are not pursued with resolution into the detailed tactical planning. Throughout the marketing planning process, constant reference back must be made, to ensure that all decisions reflect our strategic aim and that we are not dissipating effort by continuing habitual activities.

The range of services offered by the firm is the basic unit of exchange between the firm and its clients. However, clients are becoming more perceptive and demanding, facing the severe commercial pressures of today. Only if our service range continues to offer perceived satisfactions to clients' needs and problems will they continue to purchase from us.

The captive market, created by statutory audit in the UK, begins to look less secure as fee levels are questioned, business is competitively 'tendered', new types of audit are marketed and some clients, alas, cease trading altogether. In a recent article, Sir Kenneth Cork questioned whether some liquidations would have needed to occur if accountancy firms were not so hidebound in their view of their obligations in audit.

Indeed it is clear that some commercial companies, finding the traditional services of chartered accountants too limited in depth and range to meet their operational needs, are looking elsewhere. There is no shortage of 'accounting packages' of various kinds from the majority of computer software houses.

An additional problem faced by most firms arises from the simple fact that in the majority of firms the 'production' and 'sales' resources are one and the same. Thus, at a time of high workload, all staff and management are needed to do the work, and when the workload slackens, all hands are needed for selling. This 'feast and famine' cycle, well known to many firms, leaves no time for new service development or modification. Sadly, experience shows that new services do not simply evolve from the market demand. They require a conscious exercise of will.

For survival and growth depend in part on regular review and development of the range, and of individual services within the range. The fundamental objective of the review is to ensure that the services offered satisfy client needs *in the growth sectors of the market.*

In taking decisions on range, some firms have found it useful to examine their current position using a format like that shown in Form 6, a modified version of the Boston Consulting Group Matrix.

Next, taking into account the firm's marketing strategies, decisions can be made on new service development or range reduction. With new service development, either existing staff must be developed in the necessary skills or new staff possessing the necessary skills must be recruited.

Individual service development

(a) Having decided on the range, firms must consider the individual services within the range, because client needs and competitive offerings change over time.

(b) As a result, individual services tend to exhibit life cycles, passing through the four stages of introduction, growth, maturity and decline:

   (i) The introductory phasc is normally one of heavy investment in researching, creating, developing, and testing the service on the one hand; and creating client awareness and acceptance on the other.

   (ii) The growth stage involves promotion and 'distribution', during which a high quality must be maintained and a reputation established.

   (iii) The maturity stage is potentially the most rewarding as revenues and profits reach their peak. Growth slows down as market demand is saturated and competitors enter the arena. It can also be the most dangerous phase as complacency sets in and conscious observation of market trends subsides.

   (iv) If nothing is done, the service goes into decline as demand decreases and competitors introduce more effective offerings. In extreme cases, the firm can come under severe pressure as it attempts to re-vamp the service or develop replacements.

(c) While the life cycle concept clearly applies to accountancy, it is probably too general to be of practical day-to-day value. What is important is that firms recognize its implications:

   (i) Long-established, mature services (eg, audit) may remain the same in principle as they were years ago but have to change in detail to meet changing client needs.

(ii) New services may have to be developed, both to meet new clients' needs and to keep out competitors who see them as a means of ultimately acquiring the audit.

(iii) While statutory requirements impose minimum standards, there may well be opportunities to offer a range of differently priced variants for different clients and different problems.

(iv) As the current economic climate forces corporate clients to seek productivity improvements in all functions of the business; as managers in non-accounts functions become more knowledgeable in financial techniques; and as computer technology removes much of the mystique of financial analysis, so the opportunities for accountancy firms to provide both non-audit and audit-linked services increase.

One major accountancy firm in 1977 had no consultancy operation. Now it has more than 400 staff across Europe devoted to consultancy, which represents its fastest growing sector of business.

If a systematic approach is to be made to service development, the firm must set aside time to permit thorough assessment annually as part of the planning process (see Form 6).

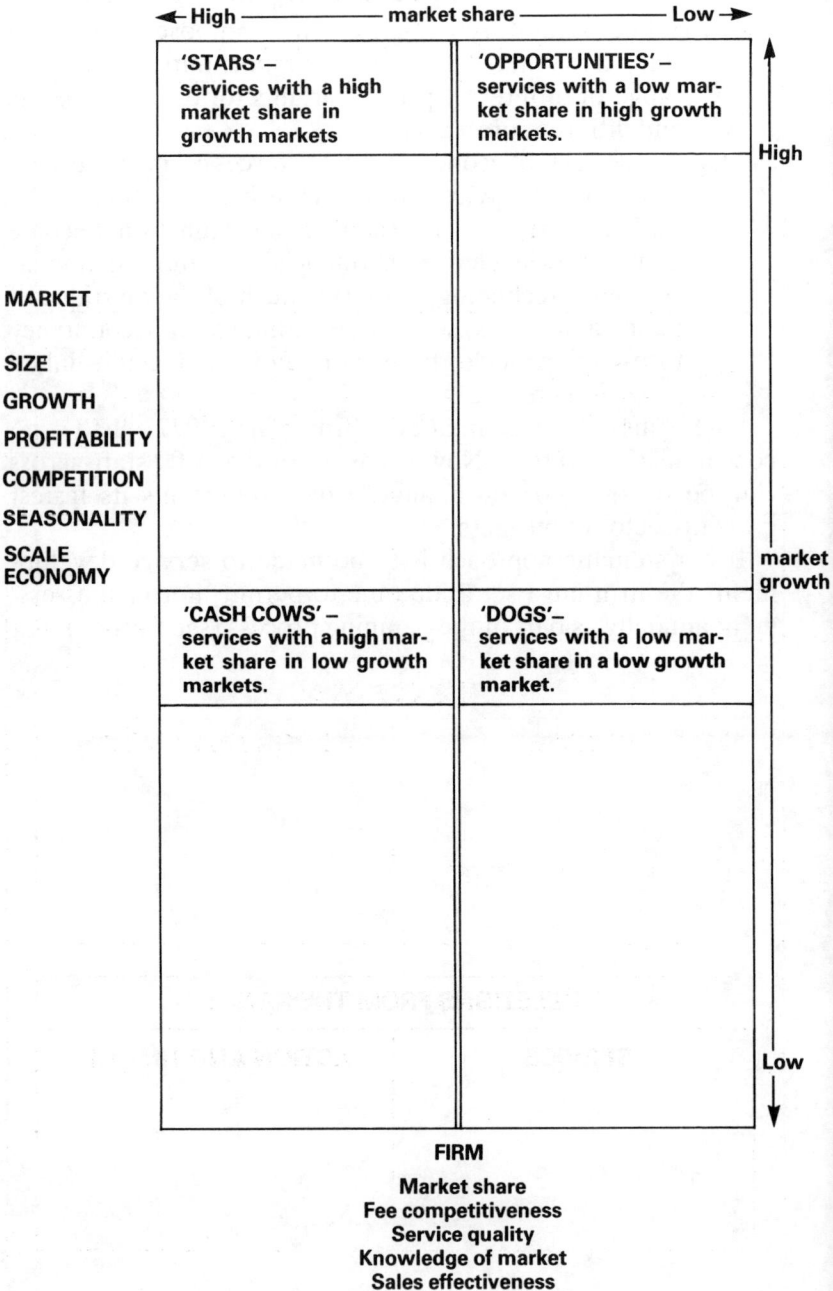

Form 6

SERVICES

◄— High ——————— market share ——————— Low —►

'STARS' – services with a high market share in growth markets	**'OPPORTUNITIES' –** services with a low market share in high growth markets.
'CASH COWS' – services with a high market share in low growth markets.	**'DOGS' –** services with a low market share in a low growth market.

High

MARKET

SIZE

GROWTH

PROFITABILITY

COMPETITION

SEASONALITY

SCALE ECONOMY

market growth

Low

FIRM

Market share
Fee competitiveness
Service quality
Knowledge of market
Sales effectiveness

Form 6A

SERVICES PLAN	
UNCHANGED SERVICES	

MODIFICATIONS TO EXISTING SERVICES	
SERVICE	**ACTION AND TIMING**

NEW SERVICES	
SERVICE	**ACTION AND TIMING**

DELETIONS FROM THE RANGE	
SERVICE	**ACTION AND TIMING**

Establishing the Firm's Fee Policy

Many firms know very little of the market view of fees. For example:

- How aware are clients of the levels of fees - the absolute levels and the hourly rates?

- How do clients perceive fees? Does, for example, a higher fee imply in their minds higher quality, or do they view fees as a commodity price with no differentiation between firms?

- Are there 'fee barriers' in a client's mind which we must avoid in any quotation for business?

- How far can we price differentially because of the perceived and accepted reputation of the firm?

- What differentials should be used on 'assignment pricing' between partners, managers and other staff?

- Is 'investment pricing' of use for major new clients where extra time is invested in the first assignment, to ensure thorough examination of the company and first-class quality, so that further repeat work is more easily identified and sold?

- How far can our fees be made more economic to the client by range selling? Can additional services be dovetailed with existing work, both to increase revenue and eliminate future selling time?

Fees are a critical area of the firm's marketing mix that tends to receive too little analytical attention.

Far too often the decision is simply to keep in line with the competition, or to work essentially on a cost plus basis.

Fees should reflect the firm's overall policy at the strategic level and show creative flexibility at the tactical level, up or down depending on the threat or opportunity.

In spite of the current pressures on fees, many firms can ease the situation by concentrating more on providing clients with the satisfactions they want, communicating the fact that it is being done, and proving that the financial value of the service is greater than its cost.

Determining fees and pricing structures

Any company or firm setting its fee levels or pricing structure must take account of its costs, the likely demand, the competitive response and the attitude of its market.

In professional service companies, fee levels may be less sensitive to these factors than in, for example, a food distributor.

The Concerns for Accountancy Firms

The primary task of the firm in setting fee levels is less to be accurate within a few pounds and more to ensure that the client gets value for money. Thus the emphasis is on setting the fee in advance, justifying it during the conduct of the assignment, and confirming its value through the quality of recommendations, and reports leading to action.

In searching for profit improvement through better pricing, the firm should also consider where it can offer enhanced value without significantly increasing its own costs.

For example, would a few more days' investigation of a client problem produce recommendations worth considerably more to the client, thereby justifying a fee which reflects not the cost of the time but the worth to the client business?

At a strategic level, the firm needs to set its fee levels in line with its overall marketing policy. For example, if its intention is to increase the number of large assignments and reduce the reliance on small ones, it may want to set a minimum fee level for small jobs which both accelerates the process and ensures that those small jobs which are undertaken do produce an acceptable return.

At a tactical level the firm will also want to consider some of the pure 'marketing' approaches to fees (see Form 7).

Planning Public Relations, Advertising and Promotion

Having decided on the markets to be served, the services to be offered, and the fees to be charged, the firm must consider how it will communicate them to actual and potential clients (see Form 8).

The major non-personal means of communication are public relations, advertising and sales promotion. Linked to these are other aspects of the firm's operation that enhance or detract from its total offering. Some are expensive, like our premises, some inexpensive but vital such as the telephonist.

Since a service is being offered, communication and distribution become almost synonymous. For example, a communications target (eg Local Chamber of Commerce) can also be a channel of distribution to a large number of potential clients.

Form 7

FEES PLAN	
OVERALL FEE STRATEGY	**ACTION AND TIMING**
SPECIFIC TACTICS	

Public Relations

The aim of public relations is to create and maintain a favourable climate of opinion in which the firm can operate. Every firm is going to have an image whether it likes it or not. It is therefore important that the actual image reflects what the firm intends in its marketing strategy.

The first task is to define those sectors where the firm wants to have a favourable reputation. Typical groups will be financial institutions (banks, insurance companies etc); other professional firms (solicitors); trade bodies (trade associations, chambers of trade); government bodies (local, national); social groups (Rotary); the media (press, local radio); potential clients, perhaps even colleges and schools.

Having identified these target groups, the next step is to find out what image they currently have of the firm:

- Do they know the firm and its services?
- What is their perception of the firm and its services?

Some of this information can be obtained by 'keeping one's ear to the ground'. If this is insufficient, formal market research may have to be undertaken. There is no reason for a great expense, since a small sample in a telephoned survey may well be adequate.

Once the present awareness and image have been identified, the firm can set its PR targets. For example, do we need to reinforce or change the present image?

Then the firm can decide which PR activities will be most cost-effective in achieving the desired image goals. Typical methods will include:

- Press publicity and developing good relationships with writers and editors.
- Membership of influential bodies, both professional and social.
- Use of a 'house style', which is consistent in all written material.
- Public speaking engagements.

Remember there are specific ethical guidelines on some of these areas, for instance a precise methodology regarding articles.

Advertising and sales promotion

There are, of course, severe limitations to the uses of advertising when applied to financial services. Advertising can be defined as communication through bought time or space. As such, it can provide information to existing and potential clients, attempt to persuade, create dissatisfaction with competitive offerings or reinforce existing purchasing habits.

However, the nature of professional services and the manner in which they are bought means that the use of advertising will always be severely limited. For example, it is exceptionally difficult to assess the best time for advertising to coincide with potential client needs.

Additionally, some ethical restrictions make substantial expenditure on advertising an innocuous activity of questionable value.

More specific plans, however, can be made for sales promotional activities. Sales promotion is primarily a tactical activity designed to advance services toward clients. Typical objectives may be:

- to introduce a new service and encourage trial;
- to display existing services to potential clients;
- to increase clients' usage of the range of services.

Opportunities for sales promotion are limited, compared with fast moving consumer goods, and would probably remain so even if the guidelines were modified. Nevertheless, there are numerous related activities which can promote or 'push' the services towards potential clients.

One clear and positive promotional tactic lies with the use of Seminars. They provide a vehicle to introduce new services and to establish the professionalism and credibility of the firm. They can ensure awareness of the full range of services available, and develop existing clients' personnel to make certain that they receive full value from systems that we may install.

Of lesser complexity, but still of importance in promotion, are the planning and structuring of the company's literature. In many firms, a great deal can be done to increase the clarity and promotional impact of brochures describing the firm's range of services.

The manner and quality of presentation of reports and proposals, even of correspondence, has promotional impact, and great care must be taken to establish a conformity of house style with the requirements of the chosen marketing strategy.

Some of the apparently minor details are of great significance in the promotion of the firm's image and services. For example, since many firms have to be largely reactive to clients, their reaction and response must be swift and positive.

Some professional service companies set specific response times within which all enquiries must be actioned. The quality of both personal and telephone reception has both immediate and lasting effect on the clients' total perception of the firm.

Thus the nature of accountancy buying and existing professional ethics limits the use of the non-personal tools of communication. Nonetheless, in today's competitive conditions, even small promotional actions can be very effective. Certainly PR has a definite role to play in creating a favourable environment in which the firm will operate.

Specific PR activities can put the firm's name to the forefront of the minds of influencers and recommenders. This systematizes an area where many firms already spend time, for example in regular liaison with such contacts as banks and solicitors, and which can expose the firm to actual and potential clients. PR with *existing* clients should not be neglected. Do they know that recommendations are welcome?

Advertising has a limited role to play, but specific limited sales promotion can have a marked effect on specific activities. Both PR and promotion should be included in the marketing plan (see Form 8).

Planning the Sales Activity

The prime focus of all promotional activity is face-to-face selling, which is the most relevant and effective form of communication for any firm offering professional services. For, by definition, professional services are people intensive: the people are the product.

The greatest opportunities both for extending existing client work and for generating new clients arise in personal interviews with client decision makers. Some firms still have a distaste for looking at this process as 'selling'. However, if a client has a particular need or problem and the firm is able to provide a relevant service which will offer a cost-effective solution, it is the accountant's duty to communicate the service as persuasively as possible. For the firm which recognizes and accepts this fact, two further stages are necessary:

- the firm as a whole should have a specific sales plan; and
- individual accountants, managers, or partners must be skilful in persuasive communication.

Form 8

PR/ADVERTISING/SALES PROMITION PLAN		
TARGET GROUPS	AWARENESS AND ATTITUDE	ACTION AND TIMING

The latter is dealt with in a later chapter. The sales plan is, however, part of the firm's marketing planning process and we should consider it here (see Form 9).

The firm has a quantified and timed statement of its total required level of fees for the planning period, usually the fiscal year. It must also assess what proportion of total fees can be expected to come in automatically and therefore the balance which will require positive selling.

This balance must then be examined against marketing strategies and broken down by service type, by marketing or industry sector, and by existing or new clients to give purpose and focus to selling.

The greatest opportunity for increased fees normally lies in selling more of the range of our services to existing clients. With current clients, the true needs are more obvious, our credibility is higher, and the amount of time needed to sell the ideas will thus be smaller, as will the selling cost.

As far as possible, the balance of business required should also be divided up and assigned to partners and managers as new business sales targets. Because clients naturally prefer professionals who can sell, rather than professional salesmen, all partners and managers responsible for clients should have sales targets agreed, even though they will not necessarily be of equal magnitude.

The targets, of course, represent only the forecast, the objective to be achieved. To complete the sales plan, the activities to achieve targets must be specified also. Thus we must know:

(a) How many proposals need to be accepted (whether formal or informal)? ie:

$$\frac{\text{Total new business fees required}}{\text{Average new business order size.}}$$

(b) How many proposals need to be submitted? ie:
No. of proposals accepted × Average conversion rate.

(c) How many enquiries must be received?

(d) How many new clients must be secured?
In which markets?
With which services?

The intention of such precise specification is twofold. First, that tactical activity should be positive and not simply responsive. Thus we ensure that tactics reflect the strategic aims

The Accountant's Guide to Practice Promotion

Form 9

SALES PLAN

NEW BUSINESS TO BE OBTAINED

INDIVIDUAL TARGETS	
NAME	**TARGET**

ACTIONS AND TIMING		
NAME	**ACTION**	**TIMING**

28

of the firm. Secondly, that by timing the activities we avoid the 'feast and famine' cycle of work, so characteristic of many service companies.

Organizing and Controlling Marketing Activities within the Firm

If results are to be achieved from all the firm's marketing work, then consideration must be given to organization of, and responsibility for the various activities. The nature of partnerships as opposed to limited liability companies raises very special difficulties here, and nowhere more than in the responsibility for, and control of, marketing activities. All the partners must be agreed on the critical importance of these actions. They must also agree on precise responsibility for the particular actions which are necessary (see Form 10).

There are clearly two distinct types of work in what has been discussed. First, the planning work such as data collection on markets, analysis and decision on objectives and strategies, and construction and communication of plans and systems.

Thus in some firms, the responsibility is given to a 'practice development' partner.

Secondly, there follows the implementation work – the contact by promotion and selling of existing and new clients which must be carried out by the whole firm. Because of the range of services, some firms have set up 'project teams' for the largest clients to supply the full range of skills and experience required to satisfy client needs.

The organizational weaknesses become apparent when examining the links between planning and implementation. In most firms, the success of marketing planning is dependent upon the goodwill and the frequency of communications between senior members of the firm, particularly if the audit practice is separated from the other main services.

Two factors seem to aid success. First, that responsibility should be concentrated rather than spread. Thus if a new service, or new market, is to be developed, it is more effective in the early stages to commit a single person or small group totally to that action. Secondly, that the activities are precisely defined, quantified, and timed at the planning stage. However, the definition must specify the links between the results desired and the activities necessary. Without such quantification, self-delusion is all too easy and the effort expended will rapidly be deflected elsewhere.

ORGANIZATION

ACTIVITIES   **RESPONSIBILITY OF:**

The Control Process

The second factor underlines the essential nature of the controls which need to be exercised. Any marketing control will measure actual performance against pre-set standards to decide when and where corrective action may be necessary.

The firm must decide first what kinds of standard are necessary. Of course we commence with results. Decisions must be made on what the firm sees as constituting success:

- What level of what profit at what time intervals?
- What level of contribution per man, group, or department?
- What level of man-hours worked by whom, by when?
- What level of chargeable hours?
- What number of assignments/contracts booked?

These questions and others provide the Results Standards, and are measured by most firms.

Controlling Causes

In marketing control, however, we must also set standards for the marketing activities; standards which will measure the *causes* of the results noted previously. For example, do we set standards for:

- the numbers of enquiries/contacts to be generated?
- the type and profile of contact needed?
- the numbers of proposals for which type of service to be submitted?
- the conversion rate to booked work to be achieved?
- the sequence of actions with major clients, particularly for extension of work and increase of business?

These standards are the crux of effective marketing in the firm. We must have the tools to assess and measure causes, to identify quickly which activities require change or greater support, so that results may be effected fast (see Form 11).

Collection of information

Sometimes this type of control will require different information from that commonly examined in a professional firm. Do we, for example, need information on:

- each enquiry/contact and its source?
- each proposal/its nature and value?
- each proposal refused and the reasons for refusal?
- levels and timing of work booked?

Form 11

CONTROLS

ACTIVITIES	STANDARD	INFORMATION TOOLS	RESPONSIBILITY OF

ACTION AND TIMING

We need a simple recording system to yield us this key information, especially, in the 'selling' activity.

It is only by collecting this information that we will refine and improve our marketing activity in the current competitive conditions.

Our quantitative analysis will define such areas as the average assignment size, average proposal size, and the new/existing client ratios. This is critical in setting realistic targets.

Causal analysis will define what cause/effect relationship exists between promotional effort, contacts gained and contracts booked. This helps us decide on the most cost-effective use of promotional time and money. Our lead time analysis – analysing the lead times between contact and proposal, and proposal and booking – is critical in deciding when sales effort must be stepped up, or when recruitment will be needed. It also has tactical use in signalling possible cash flow problems several months ahead.

Analysis of reasons for booking or refusal of work – particularly strength in, or lack of expertise, lack of knowledge of a prospective industry, high fee levels – all signal to the marketing controller possible changes necessary in the service range, the fee policy, or the training of personnel. It also provides interesting sidelights on the current activity of our competition.

Taking Corrective Action

Once we have identified these types of relationships, it becomes much easier to set diagnostic standards working backwards from the required fee revenue target.

For example:

Work required next year	£350,000	
Average assignment size	7,000	50 clients
Historic existing:		
new client ratio	46:4	4 new clients
Booked: proposed ratio	1:2	8 new proposals or £56,000 proposed to 8 prospective clients
Enquiry: proposed ratio	3:2	12 new contacts (NB:NOT one per month. Most must be made early in the year)

Our lead time analysis may tell us that these must be generated in the first six months, at which stage we are seeking five new contacts per month for January to June.

Given such a concept, with the analysis to support it, control will then monitor monthly against the standards set. Corrective action will be of two types:

What actions will sell more - more contacts?
- more proposals?
- larger proposals?
- better conversion/selling?

Where do we find more staff?

How do we ensure existing staff have appropriate skills? (see Form 12)

Control approached in this way keeps attention focused on causes rather than effects. It is only by changing causes that one can hope to change results. In reality, of course, averages and ratios vary, and sometimes causes are difficult to identify. Often random events seem to play a major part. However, one must avoid making perfection the enemy of the good, and at least control what does yield to analysis.

Planning is essentially only the thinking that proceeds action. But it needs formalizing. The plan should be in writing. The entire planning process discussed here can be documented very simply, the 12 forms shown can be used or adapted and will become the basic process to control marketing action.

But it must be your plan. A system, however good, cannot do it for you. The process must be tailored. This is for three main reasons. First, what you and your firm want to do is essentially different from others. Secondly, doing it must take account of ever changing circumstances in the market, among clients and others who may use your firm's services. And, thirdly, because of both these factors it demands a creative approach that finds and presents attractively the things that make your firm able to meet needs a little differently, and a little better, than your competitors; not in every respect, of course, but certainly in some. (If this is not true, then you are, in the longer term, likely to be in trouble.)

What has been presented in this chapter is an approach; guidelines that are intended to assist both the thinking and the action involved in promotional activity that is increasingly more necessary and must be ever more professional in accountancy.

Form 12

TRAINING REQUIRED		
WHAT	**WHO**	**ACTION AND TIMING**

Chapter 3

The Promotional Plan

'Plan the work and work the plan'

If marketing is not a euphemism for advertising nor is promotion. The word describes a number of different techniques and implies a plethora of combinations and ways of using them.

As the chart below shows, while the various techniques of promotion act to put accountants in front of prospective clients, or generate enquiries, they cannot, by their nature, produce actual fee paying clients. Only the process of sale can convert initial interest generated by promotion into actual business.

COMMUNICATIONS MIX

- Public relations
- Advertising
- Direct mail
- Sales promotion
- Selling
- The client

A brief comment about each will serve to put them into context: the aim of public relations is to create or maintain a favourable climate of opinion in which the firm can operate. Every firm is going to have an image, the question is whether it projects the right image and how strongly. It is therefore important that the actual image reflects what the firm wants. This applies equally for individual offices as for the firm overall.

The first task is to define those 'publics' among whom the firm wants to have a favourable reputation. Having identified the target groups, the next step is to find out what image they currently have of the firm:

(a) Do they know the firm and its services?
(b) What is their perception of the firm and its services?

Some information can be obtained by 'keeping one's ear to the ground'. If this is not sufficient, more formal market research may have to be undertaken.

In such cases where perception surveys have been done, and an increasing number are being conducted, the results often provide the firms involved with some sobering food for thought. For example, one firm found they were falling between two stools, being perceived as neither local, with the special knowledge that implied, nor as part of a major group with its attendant advantages. Another regular source of concern from such surveys is the ignorance of the full range of services available from a firm even among actual clients.

Once the present awareness and image have been identified, PR targets can be set, ie who should know and perceive what about the firm? The firm can then decide which PR and promotional techniques will be most cost-effective in achieving the desired image goals. Typical methods include among others:

(a) PRESS PUBLICITY AND DEVELOPING GOOD RELATIONSHIPS WITH WRITERS AND EDITORS

This does not just happen, it means taking the initiative, following up, and delivering – sticking to deadlines and so on (for example does your local radio station know if you have someone prepared to comment where appropriate?)

(b) MEMBERSHIP OF INFLUENTIAL BODIES

This does not just happen. Someone (the right person), has to belong and take part. It takes time, but can lead to good contacts, and such bodies as trade associations in industries where the firm works or wants to work should not be neglected. Contacts once obtained should be followed systematically, this may be as simple as arranging to call them rather than waiting for a call that never comes.

(c) USE OF 'HOUSE STYLE' FOR BROCHURES AND WRITTEN MATERIAL

Again it does not just happen, someone has to decide what is needed and maintain the image. Brochures are a case in point; for many practices the brochures are the same as everyone else's, out of date, introspective, boring and – most often – brown. A vital point to remember is that it is not just a case of making them look better (though this is important), getting the message right comes first and a graphic designer may not be the best person to do this.

(d) PUBLIC SPEAKING ENGAGEMENTS

These have to be sought out and you have to field the right person, ie someone who can make a presentation of a quality that will get them asked back (not whoever is most senior or happens to be available), but well done they can certainly produce enquiries.

Advertising can be defined as communication in bought space, the intention being to attract existing and potential customers to the firm and its services. it can:

(a) provide information;
(b) attempt to persuade;
(c) create dissatisfaction with competitive offerings;
(d) reinforce existing purchasing habits.

Limited budgets may preclude mass action here, although some activity may be important and some may be done collaboratively on behalf of 'accountancy' itself.

Therefore, while relaxing the rules on advertising may be used beneficially, especially by the larger firms, the 'best buy' in terms of promotional mix for the medium-sized firms will perhaps continue to be public relations and promotion, planned and followed through as well as reactive; coupled with an increasingly planned, organized, and professional sales effort.

Direct mail, promotion through the post, is another matter; essentially only a specialist form of advertising, it has considerable relevance for most firms and warrants a chapter of its own.

Sales promotion encompasses a number of elements, often used together as a 'campaign' around one particular service or at one time. The use of newsletters, events, briefings etc immediately after a budget is perhaps the best example.

More strident techniques may never pay dividends for accountants, who, as in any other business must select what is appropriate and of course work only with what is ethical.

Perhaps the area of greatest change is that of selling. Nice guys do in fact sell in some accountancy firms and certainly in many comparable fields. Nice guys who don't sell go bankrupt, or at least – in an area where some business continues to beat a path to the door – they fail to meet their growth or profitability targets (and that is bad enough).

Selling will not just happen either. To be professional, to be acceptable, it needs to be planned. The client contact run must increase the chances of business resulting from it. Yet it remains an area of weakness. Promotional activity is geared primarily to producing enquiries; consider what happens when an enquiry is received. Someone is referred, perhaps by a bank manager and telephones the firm. What happens? Is the response specifically designed to give the best impression? Who speaks to the enquirer? Who goes to visit them if appropriate? Is the action specified to increase the chances of business resulting or is it dealt with by whoever is in that day, has time or is most senior?

To ensure success it needs responsibilities, even targets, laid against individuals. Sales activity must then be deployed acceptably so that the techniques are made full use of but clients remain content; so that we run the kind of client contact we want and that clients find they like.

Certain firms already gear up sales activity and use techniques, routine in other business, to bring a sales edge to their contacts.

Overall, relaxation of rules on advertising has probably benefited the big firms and fostered the current trend towards polarization of the larger firms and the others, though the big firms may not benefit as much as they think and the market as a whole for professional advice may expand to the benefit of all including banks etc. Advertising may allow the medium-sized firm to develop small, well defined market segments, but major expenditure is unlikely to be cost-effective for what can only ever produce prospects rather than actual customers.

To date, the pace of change has not been such that the most marketing orientated practices have left the others behind, but action is necessary to close the gap. If it is delayed simply because of a distaste for change it will be found more difficult to take later rather than sooner. When it does take place, the promotional activity that follows must be persuasive. That is the nature of promotion; money spent, for example, on a brochure that is not persuasive is wasted.

Having advocated a planned approach to promotional activity, let us turn to the kind of planning involved.

The Planning Process

From the client's viewpoint, accountants appear numerous, similar, and by no means the only source of some of their services.

There are few accountants today, like the one who did not believe in promotion until he found he had to put a 'For Sale' notice outside his premises, who feel business will just arrive.

Most accept that the world is unlikely to beat a path to their door. Some form of promotion is necessary. It attracts business, preferably of specific sorts and in the required quantity, and helps make you distinctive from the competition.

Successful promotional activity needs to be based on a continuous process of review and action, and preparing and implementing a comprehensive promotional strategy demands time, skill and a systematic approach.

Perhaps the first thing to consider is who does this. The laying of responsibility is crucial. In a business where client pressure and where the democratic partnership process can make a focusing of attention more difficult, someone has to wear the 'marketing hat'. That person does not have to do everything, perhaps the reverse. What is needed is a coordinator and above all, an initiator of activity.

Many firms are beginning to alter their attitude to promotion. One firm has removed marketing, that is sales and promotional matters, from the agenda for regular partners meetings (often one suspects at the end of a busy day) and now has separate sales promotion meetings to ensure that attention is focused on these important topics.

Unless this line is pursued there is a real danger that matters will drift.

The checklist (Figure 1) makes clear 12 key points which can then be examined in more detail. They can be considered under five main sequential stage headings:

(a) Analyse the firm's needs

The prime difficulty in the analytical stage is not so much the identification of the need, but ensuring that the need is real and not imaginary.

Identification of a need can come from:
(i) formal research;
(ii) own company investigation;
(iii) professional staff;
(iv) specific market demands;
(v) our own observations.

Such analysis is part of the total marketing review (see Chapter 2). Promotionally we are primarily concerned to show clearly the interrelationship of client categories (ie the kind of firm/organization they are), products (ie the kind of work

---

PROMOTION PLAN CHECKLIST

1. Analyse market and clearly identify the exact need.
2. Ensure the need is real and not imaginary and that support is necessary.
3. Establish that the tactics you intend adopting are likely to be the most cost-effective.
4. Define clear and precise objectives.
5. Analyse the tactics available, taking into consideration the key factors regarding:
   –the market;
   –the target audience;
   –the product/services offered;
   –the firm's organization/resources.
6. Select the mix of tactics to use.
7. Check budget to ensure funds are available.
8. Prepare a written operation plan.
9. Discuss and agree operation plan with all concerned and obtain management decision to proceed.
10. Communicate the details of the campaign to those involved in implementing it and ensure that they fully understand what they must do and when.
11. Implement campaign ensuring continuous feedback of necessary information for monitoring performance.
12. Analyse the results, showing exactly what has happened, what factors affected the results (if any) and how much it cost.

Figure 1

categories involved) and business (ie new business – a new client, extension – an existing client buying more etc). We may well have to plan different strategies to impact specific areas, for example to increase tax work done for family businesses with whom we have not had prior contact.

Once a need has been clearly identified, it must be established that whatever support you intend using is likely to be the most *cost-effective method* of fulfilling that need. Then the planning stage can commence.

(b)   Preparing the operation plan for the practice
The first stage of any plan must be the *quantification of the objectives*. A clear statement of exactly what you want to

achieve stated as specifically as possible is needed. An objective which says: 'to improve audit business' is just not precise enough, whereas an objective which states: 'to improve the number of new clients buying tax services by 50 per cent this year' makes it clear to everyone exactly what needs to be done and above all *how success will be measured*.

Once the objective is finalized the *selection of tactics* can take place. This will depend on a number of factors:

(i) The market available to the practice
● What is its nature?
● Is it buoyant or is it in a low period?
● Is it price conscious? If so, how?
● What is the competition doing?
● What is the client profile?

(ii) The target audience
● Types of people/organization?
● What are their buying habits?
● What motivates buyers?
● What are their current attitudes to promotion?

(iii) The services (standard or tailored) offered by the firm
● What is its current performance?
● What are its strengths and weaknesses?
● What promotional support has it received in the past?
● Capacity available?
● Market profile/image?
● Position in life cycle? (see page 16) ie is it seen as new and interesting like certain EDP activity or old and dull, like certain standard audit work.

(iv) Organization of the firm
● What are our current sales and promotional methods?
● Would some tactics cause internal difficulties, eg in terms of administration?
● Is the firm involved in any other activity which might affect what we want to do or detract from it?

Having answered these questions there may still be a number of alternative tactics, all of which could be suitable for achieving the objective. The decision as to which to use will then depend on which is the most cost-effective.

Once the decision on tactics has been made, the details should be formalized into a written operation plan. It is always worth writing this down even in a small practice. It is not a one-off exercise but will eventually provide a reference which can be updated regularly so that it always sets out the plan for the next period. Planning of this nature is a 'rolling' process. It should include:

- background information as to why the promotional support is necessary;
- the objectives;
- a profile of the target audience(s);
- reference to service details;
- details of additional support other than that which you are actually planning, perhaps that being done by associated offices;
- budget details – how much the action is estimated to cost;
- implementation details showing exactly how the plan will be implemented;
- controls, standards and methods of obtaining results;
- an action plan, or timetable; showing what actions are required, when they should be carried out and by whom.

There are a variety of ways of making the decision on budget more logical, for example using comparisons with competitors, standard percentages of revenue and so on. (This concept is developed in Figure 2.)

(c)   Implementation preparation

Providing the operation plan has been correctly prepared, the pre-implementation preparation should be a formality.

This can only be achieved if the operation plan has been discussed and agreed with *everyone* concerned with the support activity, *well before any action is required.* This can ensure you pick up ideas (or identify snags) from everyone in the firm — some of whom may surprise you with their constructive comments.

Setting the promotional budget

There are several approaches to this, quite complex, issue.

1.   *Percentage of sales*

To take a fixed percentage based, usually, on forecast sales relies on the questionable assumption that there is always a *direct* relationship between promotional expenditure and sales.

Figure 2 Setting the promotional budget

It assumes, for example, that if increased sales of ten per cent are forecast, a ten per cent increase in promotional effort will also be required. This may or may not be realistic and depends on many external factors. The most traditional and easiest approach, it is probably the least effective.

2. *Competitive parity approach*
This involves spending the same amount on promotion as competitive firms or maintaining a proportional expenditure of total 'industry' appropriation or an identical percentage of gross sales revenue compared with competitive firms. The assumption is that in this way market share will be maintained. However, the competition may be aiming at a slightly different sector and including competition in the broadest sense is no help. If you can form a view of competitive/industry activity it may be useful but the danger of this approach is that competitors' spending represents the 'collective wisdom' of the 'industry', and the blind may be leading the blind!

It is important to remember that competitive expenditure cannot be more than an *indication* of the budget that should be established. In terms of strategy it is entirely possible that expenditure should be considerably greater than a competitor's – to drive him out – or perhaps for other reasons, a lot less.

Remember that no two firms pursue identical objectives from an identical base line of resources, market standing, etc, and that it is fallacious to assume that all competitors will spend equal or proportional amounts of money with exactly the same level of efficiency.

3. *Combining percentage of sales and competitive advertising expenditure*
This is a slightly more comprehensive approach to setting the budget but still does not overcome the problems inherent in each individual method. It does, however, recognize the need for maintaining profitability and takes into account the likely impact of competitive expenditure.

4. *What can we afford?*
This method appears to be based on the premise that if spending something is right, but the optimum amount cannot objectively be decided upon, what money is available will do.

Figure 2   Setting the promotional budget (contd)

Look at:

(a) what is available after all the other costs have been accounted for, ie, premises, staff, selling expenses etc;
(b) the cash situation in the business as a whole;
(c) the revenue forecast.

In many companies advertising and promotion are left to share out the tail-end of the budget; more expenditure being considered to be analogous with lower profits. In others, more expenditure on advertising could lead to more sales at marginal cost which in turn leads to higher overall profits.

Again not the best method, demonstrating an *ad hoc* approach that leaves out assessment of opportunities in the long and short term.

5. *Fixed sum per sales unit*
This method is similar to the percentage-of-sales approach, except that a specific amount per unit, (eg, per man-day sold) is used rather than a percentage of pound sales value. In this way, money for promotional purposes is not affected by changes in price. This takes an enlightened view that advertising expenditure is an *investment* not merely a cost.

6. *What has been learned from previous years?*
The best predictor for next year's budget is this year's.

Are results as predicted? What has been the relationship of spending to competition? What is happening in the market? What effect is it having and what effect is it likely to have in the future?

(a) Experiment in a controlled area to see whether the firm is under spending or over spending. As the chairman of a major company once said, 'I know that 50 per cent of our advertising expenditure is wasted, the trouble is I don't know which 50 per cent'.
(b) Monitor results, this is relatively easy and the results of experiments with different budget levels can then be used in planning the next step (although you must always bear in mind that all other things do *not* remain equal).

7. *Task method approach*
Recognizing the weaknesses in other approaches, a more comprehensive four-step procedure is possible. Emphasis here is on the tasks involved in the process already described of

Figure 2   Setting the promotional budget (contd)

constructing a promotional strategy. The four steps of this method are:

(a) ANALYSIS

Make an analysis of the marketing situation to uncover the factual basis for promotional approach. Marketing opportunities and specific marketing targets for strategic development should also be identified.

(b) DETERMINE OBJECTIVES

From the analysis, set clear short- and long-term promotional objectives for continuity and 'build up' of advertising impact and effect.

(c) IDENTIFY THE PROMOTIONAL TASKS

Determine the promotional activities required to achieve the marketing and promotional objectives.

(d) 'COST OUT' THE PROMOTIONAL TASKS

What is the likely cost of each element in the communications mix and the cost-effectiveness of each element?

What media is likely to be chosen and what is the target (ie, number of advertisements, leaflets etc?). For example, in advertising, the media schedule can easily be converted into an advertising budget by adding space or time costs to the cost of preparing advertising material. The promotional budget is usually determined by costing out the expenses of preparing and distributing promotional material etc.

The great advantage of this budgetary approach compared with others is that it is comprehensive, *systematic* and likely to be more *realistic*. However, other methods can still be used to provide 'ball-park' estimates, although such methods can produce disparate answers, for example:

(a)   we can afford £10,000;
(b)   the task requires £15,000;
(c)   to match competition £17,500;
(d)   last year's spending £8,500.

The decision then becomes a matter of judgement allowing for your overall philosophy and objectives.

There is no widely accurate mathematical or automatic method of determining the promotional budget. the task method does, however, provide, if not the easiest, probably the most accurate method of determining the promotional budget.

Figure 2   Setting the promotional budget (contd)

Do not forget either that if everybody feels involved they will more easily commit themselves to the next stage. In a business where your 'production', 'sales' and 'promotional' resources in terms of people are the same individuals, the way in which the tasks are shared out and the certainty of getting things done is very important.

(d)   Implementation

The success or failure of any promotional activity, providing it has been thoroughly planned, then rests on how well it is implemented. The effectiveness of the implementation will depend on how well the details are communicated around the practice and then controlled. Therefore the details of what is to be done must be communicated in such a way that they are clearly understood by everyone.

Effective methods of controlling the implementation must be set up to obtain maximum feedback while promotional activity is running. This will permit any necessary changes to be made at the earliest opportunity.

(e)   The post analysis of results

Any promotional campaign can involve a great deal of personnel time and is often expensive in terms of opportunity cost, that is time which could be spent earning fees, supervising projects or both. This is true regardless of what is spent on the other aspects.

You therefore want to know how money is being spent, and what achievements are obtained from that expenditure. Examining the detailed results of every form of promotional activity will show clearly:

- what the situation was prior to the activity;
- what we aimed to achieve (the objective);
- what the situation is after the promotional activity has ended (and what have we achieved);
- whether we entirely met our objectives and if not, why not;
- whether there are any factors outside our control which might have influenced the result, what they were, (eg competitive activity, legislation changes) and their effect;
- what has happened to the rest of the market or at least our near competitors;
- what the effect might have been had we not carried out the promotion;
- what the budget was and how it was spent.

Careful analysis of what has been achieved is important, not least as part of the planning and consideration of what we do next, which should be occuring in a continuing cycle.

No promotional activity plan can be carried out in isolation. Promotion, in a service business, involves all aspects of that business. A service business must be just that; accountants must be truly client orientated. Only if the service elements are, together, of the right level will final conversion to purchase occur. The best promotional plan we can conceive will fail if any other factors let us down. For example, a client may attend a luncheon put on by the firm and be persuaded to take an interest in services beyond those currently being used. If when he phones the office later to get more details, the switchboard handles the call badly or his contact does not have the right details to hand, the chances of his being persuaded decline.

Two key links that are vital in this way are people and administrative systems. Both need to be checked and maintained at an appropriate level, someone must ask, 'do our people − all of them − really complete that link correctly? Are they really selling, not just providing information? What is the quality of the letters they send? Are clients impressed with the response when they telephone us?' And how do you know these things? When did you last telephone your own office incognito to see how clients are really dealt with?

Similarly the systems and procedures we use also need to be geared to what is right for the client. Are procedures simple, straightforward and understandable by the client? Are any necessary details of procedure explained to them? Or is there a danger that methods and practices are not tailored to helping the client but have grown up haphazardly over the years for no good reason?

Once promotional activity has brought prospective clients to our door all the other resources we have must be actively geared to converting them into actual purchasers Sometimes things seem designed to prevent or ignore the final step rather than to increase the danger of making a sale!

Finally, bear in mind just exactly what it is the firm is promoting – not just various financial services but other reasons why clients use a chartered accountant (remember there are alternatives) and why they should use your firm in particular.

The client demands *expertise,* knowledge of tax, financial processes and guidance through the jungle of accountancy practices. He demands *objectivity,* impartial advice that appears to be telling him what is best for him (not what will make the firm the most money), and he demands *efficiency,* the time and hassle taken out of what the layman finds a complicated and perhaps uncertain process. He will use a chartered accountant only if he feels they will provide these things. He will use your firm only if he feels, or rather if you persuade him, that you will provide them better than will the alternatives.

Planning and implementing a soundly based systematic promotional plan is not easy. Nor is ensuring that all the back up resources, people, skills and systems are geared to converting the initial enthusiasm created in potential customers into actual business. But, it is certainly necessary, and done successfully provides a sound basis for securing, and more important enlarging, your business.

The Link with Sales Activity

As has been mentioned promotional activity is not only designed to produce 'leads', the raw material of sales activity, it can *only* produce leads. With experience you will be able to monitor the level of promotion necessary to produce the required number of leads, relating this in turn to the kind of formula that can be used to provide an indication of what the required number should be in a particular period.

This is not difficult, though data has to be recorded in a suitable manner for sufficient time to provide relevant historic data. Using our fee targets for the future period and historic information relating to average assignment size, the ratio of new clients needed to augment continuing work with regular clients and the ratios between work proposed and booked and the number of enquiries that do result in work being proposed, you can estimate how many enquiries we are seeking.

Regular monitoring of these latter ratios, and a watch on the trends, will often provide useful information as to how well enquiries are being handled and on the quality of proposal writing.

The example, repeated from Chapter 2 makes the point:

Work required next year	£350,000	
Average assignment size	7,000	50 clients
Historic existing:		
new client ratio	46:4	4 new clients
Booked: proposed ratio	1:2	8 new proposals or £56,000 proposed to 8 prospective clients
Enquiry: proposed ratio	3:2	12 new contacts
		(NB:NOT one per month. Most must be made early in the year)

Having generated the right number of leads it is crucial to respond to them in a way that makes the best use of them and that increases the likelihood of them progressing to actual business. In addition, realistically, some screening must go on, not all leads are equally valuable, some are time wasters, some of low potential, some seek expertise the firm does not have, or want work done in areas the firm does not wish to pursue. Until it is clearly known what priority is involved, all leads should be responded to with the same degree of consideration.

Everyone must be briefed as to how to respond to enquiries. It may be useful to have an enquiry form. This can act as a checklist, making sure the right information is collected; as a record, and as a prompt to ensure that progressing action is taken.

The rules regarding what action is taken are simple. It must be customer orientated, designed to give the right impression and progress matters appropriately. Who handles it must be dependent on sales skill as well as technical competence, and not simply a factor of who is in the office on a particular morning.

The first objective is to make sure you meet the client, giving yourself an opportunity to discover exactly what he needs and structure the whole ongoing sequence of customer contact with him in the way you want and in a manner he will find persuasive but of course acceptable.

This whole sequence, including the written proposal stage, is the subject of a later chapter. It is worth restating here, however, that is a *continuous* process. First in the sense that the conversion of enquiries takes time, numbers of meetings, visits, letters over a period of perhaps weeks and months. Many an enquiry has been jeopardized, many a job lost because of poor follow up. This process must be handled systematically and, if necessary, persistently and time found for it to fit in with 'production' responsibilities. Furthermore, once the business is booked, the process does not stop, it involves a continuous process of review and action. With existing clients every meeting should be regarded as a potential opportunity to identify new work possibilities, sow the seeds for new projects or propose new work:

Sell on   –offering new, different services to those already handled;

Sell up   –increase the value of existing work and extend the scale of involvement;

Sell across –to other parts of the client company (subsidiary locations, etc).

Seek references to other sources of work and, of course, simply repeat what you have done (next year's audit).

'Time is money' is an old cliché, but sales effort and client contact of the sort described take time. The more certainly it is carried out, the better the conversion from opportunity or prospect to firm business and the greater will be the impact on profitability.

A final point upon this area must bring us back to people and responsibility. The firm must have some sort of 'account manager' system so that someone accepts responsiblity for the process of review and continuous selling to clients, and for the progressing of each and every enquiry. In this way things will not go by default. Indeed it follows that failure to meet this responsibility once laid down is just as unacceptable as a failure in technical competence. This is explored in Chapter 7 which reviews the various techniques and tactics that will make up the activity specified in the plan to make this sort of link with sales activity possible.

Chapter 4

The Promotional Mix

**'Cast thy bread upon the waters:
for thou shalt find it after many days'**

Ecclesiastes

The 'target' chart in the last chapter set out the essence of the various techniques at the accountant's command and showed their differing roles. Now we investigate these more closely to see how they work, how they can be used and what impact they will have. Consider first the firm's overall image.

Image

Image is always important, to any organization. It can be powerfully descriptive. Think for example what a clear, detailed picture comes to mind regarding some companies just on mention of their name – Marks and Spencer, Habitat; yet what does come to mind is, on analysis, often subjective. It is image, rather than detailed factual knowledge.

It is even more important for a service which is inherently intangible, and which has a limited amount of permissible promotional techniques with which to work. Imagine Mr Smith. he needs an accountant, but he does not know one. He can look one up in a directory, but then what – is one whose name begins with 'A' better than any other? So he checks around, he asks people and finally his bank manager recommends one, or more likely two. He picks one and phones them. At this stage he still knows virtually nothing about them, but at every stage he builds an initial impression in his mind. It is cumulative, and such initial impressions may be difficult to shift.

He observes the way the phone is answered, how his call is handled, what action is suggested, what questions asked; he visits one of the partners, he notes the plate on the door, the reception, the welcome, whether he is expected or kept waiting, what is provided for him to read, whether he gets a cup of coffee. Certainly he may be impressed by the meeting, but he continues to mentally file and assimilate the other details, the brochure he was given, the follow-up letter he receives. And so on and so on, and, if the cumulative impression of all these details is poor he may question the competence, question the ability to relate to his needs, his problems. Every detail counts; if he finds only a three day old newspaper in reception he is entitled to question the efficiency of the firm. Even one detail that gives the wrong impression is too many.

The importance of all this is compounded by the fact that he may well be going through the same process with two or more firms and making comparisons. Things are getting more competitive and it is a pity if the wrong impression is given by default.

What therefore are the key issues in this area and how can you make sure they are working for you? It is as much a question of attitude as organization. To illustrate this, take for example, two positions that are key to the firm's image, the telephone switchboard and the receptionist.

The Telephone Switchboard

When was the last time you telephoned your own organization, without it being immediately clear who you were? How did the experience leave you feeling? Satisfied, pleased or perhaps dismayed? If you have not done this recently, do so soon; it could be very informative.

On every incoming call, the telephonist is the first person to whom client or prospective client speaks. The impression given is vitally important, and deserves far more attention than many give it.

A desultory mumbling of the telephone number (eventually) by way of a greeting, and then an excellent chance of being misrouted or left in a silent telephone limbo, are telphone techniques that we have all come across too often. Given the choice, we try as customers – never to repeat them. We take our business elsewhere.

A good telephonist answers promptly and politely – an overworked switchboard is no excuse for delay or rudeness and more money will go on lost business than on recruiting another telephonist. Greetings should be short, friendly, informative; '5493' is not suitable even if said with a question mark. 'Hello' is equally useless and impolite, for it invariably puts the onus on the caller to ask 'Is that Countryside Accountants?".

'Good morning, Countryside Accountants … may I help you?, said with a reasonable amount of enthusiasm is well worth the trouble. The telephonists who do this and their other tasks properly are valuable members of their firm, to be paid accordingly.

If the telephonist is required to ask the caller's name, she should be sure to use it when she puts the call through, eg 'Mr Smith, I am putting you through to Mr Brown now'.

However, it is pointless to do that if what happens next is that a phone rings on Mr Brown's desk, and Brown has to establish for himself who is calling. If the telephonist has discovered the name, she should phone Brown and say, 'Mr Smith is on the line for you, Mr Brown', before connecting them.

The good telephonist does not keep callers waiting, especially in silence. Some callers cannot hear if the phone extensions are ringing; for all they know they have been forgotten and, 'Brown' has not been called yet. Calls are expensive. If the person being called does not answer or cannot take the call, the message should be, 'I am sorry Mr Smith, but Mr Brown is not available – may I take a message?'.

If Brown is being called to the phone, the telephonist should speak to the caller frequently to reassure him, to apologize for his wait and to give him the opportunity to leave a message and ring off. Messages must be taken down carefully and accurately.

A message pad tailored to your particular firm, printed (with, if necessary, carbon copies) and on a standard size paper, perhaps A4, not only ensures messages are taken clearly, it puts an added importance on them and often removes the necessity for transcribing, as the resulting sheet can be neatly added to correspondence, a client file and so on. Very few client requests or enquiries have to go astray for the extra trouble of preparing such a form to be shown to be worth while. A formal enquiry form appears in discussion of client development in Chapter 7.

The good telephonist treats the caller with consideration. If the caller asks for a person by name, he should be put straight through unless specific instructions have been left for certain calls to be re-routed. The telephonist should know all names and functions (the internal directory should be sufficiently detailed) and know enough about the firm's affairs to avoid the re-transferring of calls.

Impressions about the firm are formed in numerous ways, many people gain their impression over the telephone. Everyone who uses it, and the switchboard operator most of all, should therefore appreciate that courtesy and consideration cost nothing.

Reception

Just as important for its 'first image' responsibility is the role of reception. As obvious as this may seem, many firms still greet clients and visitors with a cold, bare room, one stained table and a broken ashtray for furniture, yesterday's newspaper or an out of date accountancy journal for reading, and a frosted glass panel with a bell push and 'ring for attention' sign by way of a greeting. Only slightly better than the unfriendly sliding panel is the pressure of a totally bored school leaver, who taken an age to look up from her magazine, knitting or nail polish to mutter 'Yes'.

The reception area and the receptionist, the switchboard operator, the letterhead and other printed material – these are all opportunities to advertise the firm. The image they portray is the image people have of the whole firm.

The receptionist should greet callers in the same manner as the telephonist, adding a personable, cheerful countenance. She should have an up-to-date list of everyone in the firm, know where to direct callers, who to contact by telephone and how to handle impatient people.

A very common fault is to give the receptionist nothing else to do but receive, which means that often she has nothing to do at all. A caller who finds a receptionist reading, knitting or gazing blankly into space, or sees her doing so while he waits for an appointment, can hardly think of the firm as being dynamic and thriving.

Appearance is as important as attitude, which means that the receptionist should be smartly dressed and the whole reception area should have a clean, pleasant appearance. It should never be used as a 'goods inwards' department, and other staff should only be in the area if they are meeting a visitor, not conducting an internal argument about client problems or management attitudes.

The reception area should be a 'silent salesman'. In addition to the firm's printed brochures other items, perhaps a series of visually appealing photographs relating to the firm, can be on display. The reception area is also an ideal place to exhibit awards, certificates, letters of commendation, etc.

Unexpected visitors should always be seen by someone from the department concerned, if not by the very person the visitor came to see – even if it is only to explain to the visitor that an appointment is essential, and to agree a time for an appointment. If an enquiry cannot be dealt with fully, a member of staff should explain why, help the visitor as much as possible and provide him with all available literature, and ensure that an appointment is made when he will be able to get what he requires.

If it is unavoidable to keep visitors waiting for any length of time, it may create a far better impression if someone from the office, rather than the receptionist, comes to tell the visitor that he will have to wait, offers a cup of tea or coffee, something to read, and perhaps explores his needs to help brief whoever will subsequently see him. Be honest about time. Do not say there will only be 10 minutes' wait when you know full well it will be half an hour. This only guarantees 20 minutes of annoyance.

Anyone calling on a firm begins forming an impression the moment the building is seen. A potential client, even if only subconsciously, will be wondering 'Will this firm satisfy my needs?'. Since no one likes to be kept waiting, the reception area can become a most critical place for lost opportunities. Everything the firm does in its contacts with callers should try to answer the client's unspoken query with 'Yes, this firm is likely to satisfy my needs'.

Every member of the staff must recognize that the first essential in making the right impression is to gain the confidence of the buyer. A positive attitude helps here and should show itself in numerous ways:

Interest

It is hard for anyone to maintain interest in the face of indifference. Enthusiasm is infectious. People should get the impression that the firm is glad to be in contact with them – helping clients is the reason for the firm being in business, and not the tiresome interruptions which some seem to think it is.

Staff should listen to problems, ask questions, be concerned to provide satisfaction with service. A client who feels that a company is not solely interested in his money will always come back, and even higher prices are unlikely to shift his allegiance.

Courtesy

In all circumstances, staff should try to stay polite and calm, however severe the aggravation. If someone complains, apologize sincerely and do not attach qualifications or excuses to the apology. The normal reaction is to 'fight back', but the person who keeps cool invariably emerges the winner. An unreserved apology costs nothing, and it is the best way to deflate an irate complainer: besides there is often more to the matter than is assumed at initial contact. Turning away those who arrive just on closing time, or putting on an act of devastating self-sacrifice to postpone lunch by two minutes does nothing to enhance the firm's image.

Efficiency

Enquiries and queries should be dealt with quickly and effectively, even if it only means that the customer has to be contacted to be informed of a delay. No-one should ever be committed to a particular course of action without first checking that it can be fulfilled. Never make promises unless they can be kept! Personal promises, however lightly given and seemingly unimportant, must always be honoured: a promise to phone back with some information should be kept even if the information cannot be obtained as quickly as expected. It is another case of the need to put ourselves in the other person's shoes, and imagine what he expects us to do – then do it.

Loyalty

However tempting it may be to blame another person in the firm or another department when faced with the consequence of your own inefficiency or mistakes, you should always try to back the firm.

Telling people that not everyone in the firm/company is efficient, saying something like, 'Oh, I agree with you – you've no idea what it is like working in this madhouse', does nothing for the image everyone should be working so hard to create.

Attitudes of this kind do not just happen; staff must be briefed, trained and motivated. It is a continuous process, and one which, obvious though much of the foregoing may seem, is not made full use of by many firms. As such, it represents a significant opportunity to stand out from the crowd.

The Clients' Viewpoint

It has been said in other fields of business 'Don't sell products – sell benefits.' The same principle applies to accountancy.

If one gets into the habit of seeing things through the clients' eyes, you will realize you do not really sell services, you sell what clients want to buy and clients do not buy specific services or products – they buy benefits.

What are Benefits?

Benefits are what products or services do for the customer. It is not important what they are, but what they do or mean for the customer. To take an everyday example, a person does not buy an electric drill because he wants an electric drill, but because he wants to be able to make holes. He buys holes, not a drill. He buys the drill for what it will do (make holes) and this in turn may only be important to him because of a need for storage and a request to put up shelving.

Realizing this not only makes selling more effective but also easier. You do not have to try to sell the same standard service to a lot of different people, but meet each person's needs with personal benefits.

Benefits are what the services you sell can do for each individual client – the things he wants them to do for him. Different clients buy the same service for different reasons. It is important, therefore, to identify and use the particular benefits of interest to each. What a product 'is' is represented by its 'features'. What a product 'does' is described by its benefits.

If this is forgotten, then the things which are important to a client will not always be seen as important from the accountant's viewpoint, particularly, if as is likely, he has had little or no sales background. The result can, understandably, end up in a conflict of priorities thus:

Client	*Accountant*
1. *Himself* Satisfaction of his needs, eg minimizing tax, saving money, improving cash flow	1. *Himself* His firm His services His ideas
2. *His needs and the benefits which satisfy them*	2. *His services and making this client buy it*
3. *This accountant:* His firm His services His ideas	3. *Benefits to this client*
4. *Buying from this accountant*	4. *Client's needs Benefits which satisfy this client's needs*

The client is most unlikely to see things from the accountant's point of view. Everyone is, to himself, the most important person in the world. Therefore, to be successful, the accountant has to be able to see things from the client's point of view and demonstrate through his words and actions that he has done so. His chances of success are greater if he can understand the needs of the people he talks to and make them realize that he can fulfil those needs.

This is achieved essentially by the correct use of benefits. In presenting any proposition to a client, even simply recommending a service in reply to a query, you should always translate what you are offering into what it will do.

Often an accounting firm grows introspective and service orientated (this is reflected in their brochure) and gradual service development can reinforce this attitude by adding more and more features. It is only a small step before everyone is busy trying to sell services on their features alone.

When competitive firms' services are almost identical in their performance, it can be difficult to sell benefits, since all seem to offer the same benefits. Choice then often depends on the personal appeal of some secondary feature. But even then, there must be emphasis on the benefits in those features, rather than on the features themselves. Features are only important if they support the benefits that the customer is interested in.

Deciding to concentrate on benefits is only half the battle, however. They have to be the right benefits. In fact, benefits are only important to a client if they describe the satisfaction of his needs.

Working out the needs, and then the benefits, means being 'in the customer's shoes'.

Who is the Client – What are his Needs?

To know what benefits to put forward, you must understand the needs of the client, and the potential clientele. Firms often have more than one decision maker, therefore it is essential to pinpoint your contact within the hierarchy in order to relate to them accurately.

To do this it is useful to analyse service in terms of features and benefits thus:

Benefit	*Feature*
provides a quicker more certain analysis with less disruption of the accounts department	computer-assisted audit

Such an analysis (and it is a useful exercise to work this out point by point), will help differentiate between features and benefits. It is a useful ploy to present the benefits first; where features lead, ie, '... we can offer a computer-assisted audit' the client response (mentally if not spoken) can too often be 'so what'.

An analysis can be produced for each service or for a service range, and can be presented within a firm to help everyone learn just what is a feature and a benefit.

Note that not all the needs will be objective ones; most buyers also have subjective requirements bound up in their decisions. Even with technical services the final decision sometimes can be heavily influenced by subjective factors, perhaps seemingly of minor significance, once all the objective needs have been met.

By matching benefits to individual client needs, you are more likely to make a sale, for the benefits of any service must match a buyer's needs. The features only give a product the right benefits.

By going through this process for particular services and for segments of the range, and matching the factors identified to client needs, a complete 'databank' of information from the client viewpoint can be assembled.

With the competition becoming increasing similar, more buyers quickly conclude that their main needs can be met by more than one firm. Other needs then become more important. If, for instance, a buyer needs tax advice he is likely to find a number of firms which will offer the service required, all of which will cost practically the same.

The deciding factors may then become people, availability, service, specialist knowledge and so on. The accountant must therefore look at the 'features' contained by the firm as a whole and be ready to convert them into benefits to clients – in the same way as we can practise finding benefits for the full service range.

All aspects of the 'features', whether to do with the services themselves, the manner in which they are provided by the firm or its staff, are sources of benefits to clients. Such factors include:

- price/fee levels
- availability of service or staff
- credit
- expertise
- specialist knowledge
- speed of action
- training assistance
- quality/objectivity of advice
- time firms have been established
- reputation, location, philosophy, size, policies, financial and international standing
- the character, style and manner of its staff

Each item listed above could be a source of benefit to potential clients and help convert them to an actual client. By 'thinking benefits' and by seeing things from the clients' point of view you can increase the contribution made to sales and the firm's profitability.

A final hazard, which can destroy client orientation is jargon. This comes in two main forms, both of which can confuse clients:

(a) *Technical accounting jargon*. You should usually let the client be first to use it, because there is always the possibility that the client will not know what you are talking about, or will form the wrong impression, yet will hesitate to admit it.

(b) *Internal jargon*. It is even more important to avoid internal jargon, for here the client, especially the new one, will be on very unfamiliar ground. Internal jargon can affect everything you deal with, and even simple phrases can cause trouble. For example, service is one area for potential misunderstanding. Promising 'immediate action' might, in your terms, mean getting something to the client within a week. He is almost bound to get the wrong impression, unless it is stated more specifically.

Knowing how and why clients view your services as they do, is a prerequisite to improving all the specific communication areas reviewed in this book and to making your own use of them more effective. This concept is revisited in the chapter on personal selling.

With this in mind we will return to the forms of promotion.

Written Promotion

Not only is there a continuous projection of image through what exists in print about the firm – from business card to brochure – but there is also a range of much more specific promotional and sales objectives implied by many items such as brochures.

Design, preparation and particularly writing these items is crucial, well worth some time and money and possibly some professional assistance. One firm who my own company recently assisted with the rewriting and design of their corporate brochure felt it worthwhile to add half as much again to a print bill of between £3-4,000. This does not mean small inputs from outside, at less cost, are impossible, they are not, and they can help.

The total process is, perhaps surprisingly, complex. One company, who knows a thing or two about work in this kind of area, use a chart to illustrate the process to those with whom they work. It shows the sequence of events involved in producing a brochure intended for recruitment purposes. The complexity and importance of detail is immediately apparent. Only by handling such a project systematically will the end result stand a chance of achieving its objectives.

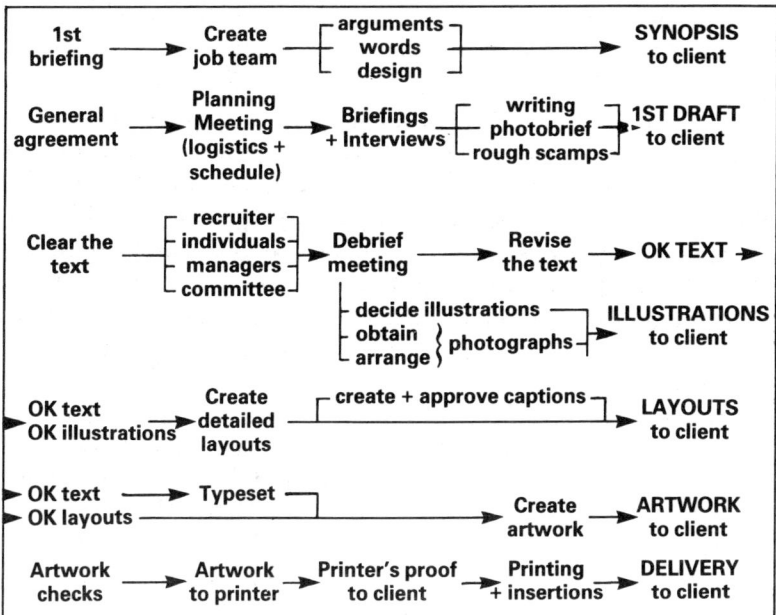

Figure 1   Publishing Process

Every product is different but this flow chart acts as a rule of thumb for planning a job-specific schedule.

Reproduced with the permission of Publishing Resources Limited of Cambridge

Getting Things Into Printed Form

You may well do all this yourself, liaising direct with a printer. On the other hand you may need professional assistance. Assistance may be needed with copy (the words used in the material), with design and graphics (how the material will look); artwork must be prepared for a printer to work from; a printer and printing process must be selected and proofs checked; colours matched etc.

In either case the process of choosing the right assistance is crucial. In selecting a printer, describe the job you want done, look at work he has done before, ask how long it will take. As much of the print business works on a jobbing basis it may be useful to know how much of the work he will do himself. With an agency or freelancer on the 'creative' side, who will be concerned with design, graphics, copy etc, you are really seeking a partner in the implementation of a part of your marketing strategy. Again look at what they have done in the past and for whom. Ask how well it worked, has that client come back to them for more, can you check personally with a satisfied client? Making the right choice is an important decision, and it may well be worth seeing a number of people. Final judgement may well be influenced by those elements of the job with which you need most help; for example the fact that it is easier to find someone who will make a brochure *look nice* than someone who will ensure its overall message, the words and way it is presented meets your objectives, and is therefore able to do a really persuasive job on those who see it.

A number of printed items are especially important.

Brochures

Brochures are designed to act in your absence, perhaps as a reminder of a meeting, perhaps to those with no other knowledge of the firm. Some have a specific purpose, to support a graduate recruitment programme, to introduce a new service, for example an EDP section. Others are more general and intended only to tell any prospective client 'all about the firm'.

Sometimes these two uses of brochures overlap and a firm, particularly the smaller firm, has one brochure intended to do all these jobs, recruit staff, persuade clients and so on.

This is an area of increasing professionalism, and great care is needed in defining the objective, creating the right message and making sure the brochure looks good and reflects the image the firm intends to project. The days of the bland, general brochure, very similar to those of other firms, describing the chronological history of the firm and everything it does, and intended to be used for everything is rapidly passing. What is needed is the ability to support contact in each particular area with something *specifically* designed for the particular job. This may mean separate brochures for recruitment and client usage, it may mean the 'corporate' brochure is a folder with separate inserts aimed at different target groups or different types of client, or it may mean a revised brochure every year. It may even mean a difference between the sort of brochure that is right to give a prospective client after a preliminary meeting and the sort suitable to present to an intermediary, eg another provider of financial services, such as a bank manager.

Overall what must be created is something accurately directed at a specific group, with a clear objective in mind, and – above all – that is persuasive. This may seem basic; promotional material is there to inform but it must do so persuasively; that is its prime purpose. The profession has had a tendency in the past to produce material that, while no doubt ethical, is so circumspect as to be largely ineffective. This does not mean moving to something that is inappropriately strident, (which might in any case be self-defeating); it does mean a greater emphasis on client need and benefits (what services do for people, rather than what they are).

Essentially a less introspective approach, better designed to its purpose, is the rule. What does this mean?

- a front cover that has the name of the firm clearly shown, and/or that makes some offer of benefit. The reader must be clear, at a glance, why he should read on.
- leaflets are expensive, so you cannot afford to waste space. there is, or should be, lots to say about the services you provide.
- it should make clear how a reader makes contact with the firm, this is, after all, the whole purpose of the communication.
- photographs, or any illustrations, should be clear, captioned if appropriate, and have some bearing on the content.
- above all the text must be truly orientated to the client,

their view, their needs, and persuasively and attractively written.

There are few rules to be observed about brochures, and those one might define are made to be broken, this is because they must be *creatively* constructed to reflect the image of the firm graphically, and aim their chosen message directly at the group involved.

Letters

The volume of paper produced in business is incalculable – memos in triplicate, invoices in quadruplicate, letters, confirmations, orders, reports, tenders, complaints ... and forms, forms and forms.

No wonder that individual letters become diluted by the sea of paper around them and command little attention. The major consideration has become to move paperwork on as fast as possible before the next lot arrives: to deal with it, to file it (though 90 per cent of it will then never be referred to again) – or preferably destroy it quickly.

Therefore it is well worthwhile considering how to attract the best attention from what you write. Unless awareness is maintained there is a danger that writing becomes routine, letters and documents being compiled on 'automatic pilot' and without any consideration of how it can be made persuasive. Many kinds of letter need to have a persuasive element:

- letters accompanying brochures;
- letters accompanying proposals;
- letters answering or following up complaints
- post audit management letters etc

and even more simple letters, perhaps confirming an appointment.

No matter what the subject of the letter is, it must:

(a) command attention;
(b) be understood; and
(c) be acted upon

(it is the last point that differentiates sales or persuasive communication from simple factual communication). If they are to do this, you have to take some care in preparing them; in this age of dictating machines, rush and pressure, it is too easy to just 'dash them off'.

Preparing persuasive 'sales' letters

Before a letter is drafted, remember the principles of selling, and in particular remember to see things through the client's eyes. Then ask five questions:

(a) For whom is the letter and its message intended? (This is not always only the person it is addressed to.)

(b) What are their particular needs?

(c) How does our service or proposition satisfy those needs – what benefits does it give?

(d) What do you want the client to do when he receives the letter? Each letter must have a clear objective, and these objectives must be:

    (i) commercially worthwhile, within the firm's overall strategy;

    (ii) stated in terms of client needs;

    (iii) realistic and achievable with available resources;

    (iv) specific, clear and time bounded; and

    (v) capable of evaluation with a Yes/No answer.

(e) How does the client take this action?

The last two questions are frequently forgotten, but they are very important. It should be perfectly clear in your own mind what you want the recipient to do and this must then be put equally clearly to the client. But even having achieved this, we can lose the advantage if lack of information makes it difficult for the client to understand exactly how he takes the action.

The principal object of writing a 'sales' letter is to draw the reader's attention to the reasons *why* he should take action and explaining what benefits he will gain is of paramount importance. It is therefore essential that we know for whom the letter and its message are intended.

The client's reasons for buying the benefits he will gain must be related to his position in the client organization and what the service does for him, rather than what the service itself is. Description of the service and what its features are is one of the functions of the leaflets, or brochures, which often accompany letters to new contacts.

Criteria for Successful Persuasive Letters

Perhaps before anything else, a persuasive letter must be attractively laid out, grammatically correct and well typed. That will at least give the impression it has originated in an efficient and reputable firm. Any company selling a service must try particularly to convey neatness and efficiency as a cornerstone of its image, and is inevitably let down by sloppy letters.

The most important part of a letter is the first sentence. It will determine whether or not the rest of the letter is read.

People seldom read a letter in the same sequence in which it was written. Their eyes flick from the sender's address to the ending, then to the greeting and the first sentence, skim to the last – and then, if the sender is lucky, back to the first sentence for a more careful reading of the whole letter. So the first sentence is about the only chance we have of 'holding' the reader, and it should arouse immediate interest.

But gimmicks should be avoided. They invariably give the reader the impression of being talked down to. So what makes for the best opening?

The Opening

Write out the name of the person you are writing to. Seeing it written down will help you visualize his point of view. Always address the letter to a person rather than to 'Dear Sir'. It is much less formal, everyone likes hearing his own name, unless we write 'personal' on the envelope there is no fear that the letter will lie unanswered in his absence.

Keep references short and subject headings to the point – his point. Do not use 'Re'.

Make sure the start of the letter will:

(a) command attention;
(b) gain interest; and
(c) lead easily into the main text.

For example ask a 'Yes' question; tell him why you are writing to him particularly; tell him why he should read the letter; flatter him (carefully); tell him what he might lose if he ignores the message; give him some 'mind bending' news (if you have any).

The Body of the Letter

The body of the letter runs straight on from the opening. It must consider the reader's needs or problems from his point of view. It must interest him. It must get the reader nodding in agreement – 'Yes, I wish you could help me on that'.

On course you are able to help him. In drafting, write down what you intend for him and of course list the benefits, not features, and in particular benefits which will help solve that problem and satisfy that need.

You have to anticipate his possible objections to your proposition in order to select your strongest benefits and most convincing answers. If there is a need to counter objections, then you may need to make your letter longer and give proof, eg comment from a third party, that your benefits are genuine. However, remember to keep the letter as short as possible.

It is easy to find yourselves quoting technicalities to the client, rather than selecting just one or two benefits which will be of particular use to him in his situation, and which support the literature.

The aims are the following:

(a) To keep the reader's immediate interest;
(b) Keep that interest with the best benefit;
(c) Win him over with second and subsequent benefits;
(d) Obtain action by a firm close.

The letter ending

In drafting you can make a (short) summary of the benefits to him of your proposition. Having decided what action you are wanting the reader to take, you must be positive about getting it.

It is necessary to nudge the reader into action with a decisive close. Do not use:

'We look forward to hearing',
'I trust you have given ...',
'...favour of your instructions',
'...doing business with you',
'I hope I can be of further assistance',

which are just phrases added as padding between the last point and 'Yours sincerely'. Where you want to prompt action you must finish in a specific manner, for example:

(a) ask him to telephone or write (or say what you will do);
(b) give him some sort of prompt to action now rather than later (perhaps while a member of staff suggested for the project is available).

Finally sign the letter yourself whenever possible, and consider letting your secretary use her own name rather than 'pp' if you are not able to sign.

If you use a postscript make sure it is a final benefit – an extra help to closing. Remember a PS gets read, so do not regard it as just for omissions but consider how you can use it, for emphasis. Like footnotes people really do read them!

Many people have acquired a habit of artificiality in writing, approaching it quite differently from their way of talking to a client, and in a way that lessens the danger of obtaining the commitment they want.

Language is important too, to the tone, feeling and acceptance of the message. This is commented on in the next section as part of a consideration of those crucial documents, proposals.

We return to the question of letters in the chapter on direct mail; and proposals, another key element of written persuasion are examined in the chapter on personal selling.

Advertising

Though some advertising has of course been permissible for some time, for example recruitment advertising and publicity for certain 'product' areas such as a publication or seminar, it is one area where the changes in ethical rules have had most effect.

The role of advertising is still sometimes misunderstood in the profession. Leaving the ethical debate on one side for the moment, let us review some of the essentials of advertising and put them into context in the whole range of techniques (some of which may still be prohibited by ethical rules).

First a definition: advertising is 'any paid form of non-personal communication directed at target audiences through various media in order to present and promote products, services and ideas'. More simply, it can be called 'salesmanship in print or film'.

The role of advertising, as one of a number of variable elements in the communication mix, is 'to sell or assist the sale of the maximum amount of, in this case the service, for the minimum cost outlay'.

There are a variety of forms of advertising, depending upon the role it is called upon to play among the other marketing techniques employed, in terms of both types of advertising and the target to which it is directed. These include by way of example:

- National advertising;
- Retail or local advertising;
- Direct mail advertising;
- Advertising to obtain leads for salesmen;
- Trade advertising;
- Industrial advertising.

A more specific way of understanding what advertising *can* do is to summarize some of the major purposes of advertising or objectives that can be achieved through using advertising in particular ways. A representative list, though by no means a comprehensive one, is as follows:

- To inform potential customers of a new product or service*;
- To increase the frequency of use*;
- To increase the use of a product/service*;
- To increase the quantity purchased*;
- To increase the frequency of replacement*;
- To increase the length of the buying season*;
- To present a promotional programme*;
- To bring a family of products together*;
- To turn a disadvantage into an advantage*;
- To attract a new generation of customers*;
- To support or influence a franchise dealer, agent or intermediary*;
- To reduce brand substitution by maintaining brand loyalty*;
- To make known the organization behind the product/service (Corporate Image Advertising)*;
- To increase the strength of the entire industry*;
- To stimulate enquiries*;
- To give reasons why wholesalers and retailers should stock/promote a product;
- To provide technical information about a product/service*.

There are clearly many reasons behind the advertising that we see around us. They are not mutually exclusive of course and many of those listed apply – or could apply – to accounting services, particularly those marked *. Whatever specific objectives the use of advertising seeks to achieve, the main purpose is usually to:

- gain the customer's attention;
- attract customer interest;
- create desire for the product or service; and
- prompt the customer to buy.

Advertising is therefore primarily concerned with attitudes and attitude change; creating favourable attitudes towards a product or service should be an important part of the advertising effort. Fundamentally, however, advertising also aims to sell, usually with the minimum of delay, but perhaps over a longer period, in the case of informative or corporate (image-building) advertising.

Any advertisement should relate to the product or service, its market and potential market: and, as a *communicator* it can perform a variety of tasks. It can:

provide information

This information can act as a *reminder* to current users, or it can inform non-users of the product's existence.

attempt to persuade

It can attempt to persuade current users to purchase again, non-users to try the product for the first time, and new users to change brands or suppliers.

create cognitive dissonance

This means advertising can help create *uncertainty* about the ability of current suppliers to best satisfy a need. In this way, advertising can effectively persuade customers to try an alternative product or brand. (In terms of the Institute's rules, this technique would appear to come under the heading 'knocking copy' – which is specifically prohibited.)

create reinforcement

Advertising can compete with competitors' advertising (which itself aims to create dissonance), to reinforce the idea that current purchases best satisfy the customer's needs.

Moreover, advertising aims to reduce the uncertainty felt by customers immediately following an important and valuable purchase, when they are debating whether or not they have made the correct choice.

Types of Advertising

There are several basic types of advertising and these can be distinguished as follows:

Primary

This aims to stimulate basic demand for a particular product type, for example, insurance, tea or wool. This has already been the subject of some experiment in accountancy.

Selective

This aims to promote an individual brand name, such as a brand of toilet soap or washing powder which is promoted without particular reference to the manufacturer's identity.

Product

This aims to promote a 'family' branded product or range of

related brands where some account must be taken of the image and interrelationship of all products in the mix.

Institutional
This covers public relations-type advertising which, in very general terms, aims to promote the company name, corporate image and the company services.

Advertising Media and Methods

There is a bewildering array of available advertising media. Here are some of the most popular methods of advertising, with a guide as to how they are used:

Daily newspapers often enjoy reader loyalty and hence, high credibility. Consequently, they are particularly useful for prestige and reminder advertising. As they are read hurriedly by many people, lengthy copy may be wasted.

Sunday newspapers are read at a more leisurely pace and consequently greater detail can be included.

Colour supplements are ideal for advertising, but appeal to a relatively limited audience.

Magazines vary from quarterlies to weeklies and from very general, wide-coverage, journals to very specialized interests. Similarly, different magazines of the same type (eg fashion) appeal to different age and socio-economic groups. Magazines are normally colourful and often read on a regular basis.

Local newspapers are particularly useful for anything local, but are relatively expensive if used for a national campaign. They are sometimes used for test market area advertising support.

Television is regarded as the best overall medium for achieving mass impact and creating an immediate or quick sales response. It is arguable whether or not the audience is captive or receptive; but the fact that TV is being used is often sufficient in itself to generate trade support. Television allows the product to be demonstrated, is useful in test marketing new products because of its regional nature, but is very expensive.

Outdoor advertising lacks many of the attributes of press and television but it is useful for reminder copy and a support role in a campaign. Strategically placed posters near to busy thoroughfares or at commuter stations can offer very effective long life support advertising.

Exhibitions generate high impact at the time of the exhibition but except for very specialized ones, their coverage of the potential market is low. They can, however, perform a useful long-term 'prestige' role.

Cinema with its escapist atmosphere, can have an enormous impact on its audience of predominantly young people; but without repetition (ie people visiting the cinema once every week) it has little lasting effect. It is again useful for backing press and television, but for certain products only, bearing in mind the audience and the atmosphere.

Commercial radio playing popular music for young people, offers repetition and has proved an excellent outlet for certain products. It is becoming apparent that the new local radio stations appeal to a wide cross-section of people and thus offer 'support' potential to a wide range of products.

Direct mail offers great flexibility for the advertiser. It is particularly useful for assisting special promotions in certain regions (national coverage of the consumer market being very expensive), and in the industrial and service field where it can be tailored to suit a very specialized audience. Direct mail is so popular in industrial marketing that the major emphasis is on producing a mail shot that is sufficiently different to be noticed and read. The other fundamental problem is the wastage caused by inaccurate and out-of-date mailing lists.

Not all media outlets will be appropriate to the nature of the business involved in a professional practice; some are still specifically excluded from use.

Before finalizing any advertising plans it may be useful to check to see what media decision will be best. You can run such a check by listing the alternative media options and putting down the advantages and disadvantages of each alongside.

This not only acts as a prompt but also gives you on one sheet of paper a summary document which will assist in making the final decision on a logical basis. This concept can be employed whatever advertisement(s) you consider placing.

The following shows one example (relating to recruitment advertising). The blank format can be used for a specific situation of your own. Media selection is a complex technical business where professional advice is probably essential, however Figure 2 is intended to provide a basis for some decision.

Figure 2 Choosing the most appropriate media for your advertisement

MEDIA	ADVANTAGES	DISADVANTAGES
1 National Dailies and Weeklies	– large circulation – minimum delay before advertisement is published – proofs supplied to enable final advertisement to be changed or mistakes corrected – specialist staff frequently available to give advice	– typesetting variable in paper set advertisements – expensive – your advertisement competing with large number of others
2 Local Daily Evening and Weekly News- papers	– attracts local people and so avoids waste – costs lower than nationals – minimum delay before publication – acts as a guarantee back-up to a national advertisement at little cost	– would not be seen by good candidates outside circulation area – specialist jobs unlikely to draw sufficient number of applications – may not be seen by senior people
3 Trade Specialist Magazines	– usually inexpensive compared with national newspapers – seen by specialist readership if you are only intending to address this group, eg those in specialist industry	– long delays between each issue frequently one month – advertisments often not seen by target audience for weeks after publication – job advertisements rarely featured prominently – not usually regarded by senior people as a primary source of jobs
4 Specialist Selection Agency Publica- tions of Candidate Lists (Recrui- ment only)	– very cheap or free – large number of specialist categories to choose from – quantity available useful guideline to whether spending money on advertising will be worthwhile	– lists usually made up of professional job hunters/job hoppers – facts often suspect or, like estate agents' house descriptions, the truth is embroidered

Figure 2 (contd)

MEDIA	ADVANTAGES	DISADVANTAGES
5 Commercial Radio and Television	– very wide coverage especially at peak listening hours – speeds of acceptance of advertisement and broadcast – impact – more people listen to radio and watch television than read newspapers – gain attention of those not necessarily thinking of using/ changing accountants and therefore less likely to notice advertisements in newspapers	– usually very expensive – cost usually means insufficient information can be provided – risk of not being seen or heard by those available during evening or at weekends
MEDIA	ADVANTAGES	DISADVANTAGES

Trade Advertising

It is often not sufficient to advertise to consumers alone, particularly as it is important that distributors are willing to stock and promote a product.

Certainly the sales force has a prime role to play in ensuring that stocking and promotion objectives are achieved. However, trade advertising also has an important role to play in this respect:

It can remind distributors about the product in-between selling calls.

It can keep distributors fully informed and updated on developments and changes of policy.

It can also alleviate problems associated with the 'cold-call' selling of less known products.

Trade advertising is usually confined to specialist trade publications and the use of direct mail communications from the company to its distributors.

Most trade advertising occurs *prior* to major consumer advertising campaigns to help ensure the buying-in of stock in anticipation of future demands to be created by the consumer advertising.

Thus, when new products are launched, or special promotions introduced, trade support is often achieved through special offers ('13 for the price of 12') or increased (introductory) discounts, all of which trade advertising can effectively emphasize.

This type of advertising can also communicate to the trade the advantage of new products as well as the timing and 'weight' of advertising support which is to come.

There is a distinct parallel here with intermediaries who are of course important to the accountancy profession and to whom messages can be directed specifically and separately, in order to influence them.

It will be interesting to see whether, now advertising is permitted, some of it is directed towards closely targetted groups such as banks and other key intermediaries.

Having reviewed something of the general principles of advertising, we must now turn to its application for professional services.

Advertising Professional Services

In many ways this sort of advertising is no different from any other but there are certainly key factors that have been found important, and will apply to the advertising that will now take place in the accountancy profession. Key factors include:

(a) *Unlike consumer advertising, much advertising of financial services will play a secondary role to that of personnel selling.*

Such advertising aims to create awareness, stimulate interest and generate enquiries for further information or personal contact. It is in fact true to say that in accountancy advertising will never actually sell anything. It only makes the later stages easier and more cost-effective; it provides the raw material for selling by producing leads or enquiries.

Direct mail, one of the most effective techniques in other fields for providing this effect, has now been added to permitted techniques.

(b) *Less money is likely to be spent on advertising financial services* than many mass appeal consumer goods because most accountancy services can be advertised more selectively to more defined markets. There are in fact, not surprisingly, fewer potential buyers for accountancy than toothpaste.

(c) *The buying decision and communications problem is different to consumer advertising.*

Consider the constraints which face the buyers of accountancy services. They need to achieve cost targets, they need to justify the purchase to others: colleagues, the board and shareholders for example.

Clearly, several people within one organization may be involved in the decision to purchase financial services and thus the advertising message may have to compromise between detailed information for one and a more general statement of facts which clearly relate to the company's problems and how they can be solved.

The potential market for accountancy services can be smaller and more specialized than consumer markets, and, therefore, media must be chosen very carefully and selectively if advertising is to communicate effectively to a good percentage of prospect companies and a large number of buying influencers without undue waste.

Mass circulation newspapers and magazines can be used again on a selective basis. Such journals can help create and maintain a required image, and also create the opportunity of communicating to 'unknown' or less definable members of a potential market, and to intermediaries. No matter how skilled and expert the analysis and interpretation of background information has been, there will always arrive the stage at which the advertisement must be appraised by a combination of logic, the known background data and sheer judgement.

We must pre-suppose that the analysis of the market has led to a sensible choice of media and advertising strategies and that these have been communicated to whoever is going to produce the advertisement.

At its best the advertisement strategy statement is brief and economical and does its job in three paragraphs:

- The basic proposition – the promise to the client – statement of benefit, to whom!
- The 'reason why' or support proof justifying the proposition, the main purpose of which is to render the proposition as convincing as possible.
- The 'tone of voice' in which the message should be delivered – the image to be projected, and not infrequently the picture the client has of himself/herself which it could be unwise to disturb, or indeed wise to capitalize on.

In other fields some of the finest and most effective advertising has sometimes been produced without reference to an 'advertising strategy' or for that matter without knowledge of market facts. However, although research cannot always give all the details, or for that matter always be infallibly interpreted, it can give strong indications and reduce the chances of failure.

Most executives, when faced with a rough or initial visual and copy layout, have an automatic subjective response. 'I like it/I don't like it', and while the creator may attempt to explain that the appraiser is not a member of the target audience, it is obviously difficult to be objective.

Nevertheless, whilst an attempt must be made to be objective, there are few experienced advertising or marketing executives who can say that their 'judgement' has never let them down. Advertising remains as much art as science. This will no doubt be true for accountancy as for other products and services.

The questions which you must ask are:

- Does the advertisement match the strategy laid down?
- Does the advertisement gain attention and create awareness?
- Is it likely to create interest and understanding of the advantages of a particular service?
- Does it create a desire for the benefits and conviction of the need to buy?
- Is it likely to prompt potential clients to action?

In other words, does the advertising communicate? Will people notice it, understand it, believe it, remember it and buy it?

The pre-test of advertisements, even on a comparatively informal scale, can often pay dividends.

Corporate Image or Identity Development

An important area where accountants can, and now will in some cases, use advertising is to build and clarify the firm's corporate image. This process begins with a name but extends to other visual features, eg typography (sometime called logo design), colour, design, slogans. These provide a foundation from which other advertising can work and thus assist in creating, stimulating and maintaining demand.

Among the arguments in favour of clear corporate image (what would be called branding in product marketing) are the following:

- Memory recall is facilitated, leading to more rapid initial buying action or greater frequency of buying, thus creating deeper loyalty;
- Advertising can be directed more effectively and linked with a 'common vein' to other company communications programmes;
- A clear image leads to a more ready acceptance of a product by intermediaries;
- The importance of price differentials, particularly *vis-a-vis* competition may be diminished;
- Additional services may be introduced more readily;
- The amount of required personal persuasive selling effort may be reduced;
- A clear image makes market segmentation easier, ie different approaches may be developed to meet specific categories of client.

Because of the need to clarify the range of tasks and techniques involved in advertising and because the present rule relaxations are in major part concerned with it, advertising has taken perhaps more than its fair share of space in this section. It should be remembered that what is necessary to ensure a successful promotion campaign is the right mix of different promotional techniques. Some, like direct mail which has proved very effective in marketing other professional services, are only recently permitted. Others, even as simple as producing an effective brochure, may be a better option especially for the smaller firm. The effect on the market of campaigns by the larger firms and what responsive action this may necessitate remains to be seen. Certainly the ability to indulge in advertising should not negate action in the other areas; ultimately, what will need to be discovered is the mix which, for any individual practice, has the most cost-effective impact on the process of securing new business.

Management Letters/Newsletters

These two categories of communication are worth separate comment.

The first, management letters, which I use to describe the kind of letter sent after an audit summarizing and making specific suggestions for the future, are often lost opportunities. Of course the formal summary and the checklist of actions for the future is important, this is perhaps the last stage of a project like an audit. In promotional terms it is also the first stage of what we intend to do next; thus there are three elements: summary, checklist for future action and proposal (or even hint of proposal) for future involvement. These do not necessarily need to go in one document; it could be in various forms, a letter and attachments for example. Certainly the third element needs to be there, written persuasively and then followed through in subsequent meetings and contacts. All the principles of making written communications persuasive mentioned earlier then apply.

Similarly, for newsletters or the kind of document that goes out after a budget or sometimes even to celebrate the opening of a new branch office, these also should be promotional documents. They do not only exist as a service to inform clients, though this is important, but to assist particular promotional objectives such as the selling of the range of services.

In both cases a clear identification of the objectives before the message is finalized is important, and because like so many of the promotional tactics available they will not individually do a complete job, the link to follow up action is crucial.

Public Relations Activity

Public relations can provide a planned, deliberate and sustained attempt to achieve understanding between you and your publics. Not just understanding, but understanding that whets the appetite for more information, that in fact prompts enquiries, re-establishes dormant contracts and reinforces your image with existing clients.

Not only is public relations activity (PR) potentially a powerful ally in your promotional armoury, it is also free. Well, it is compared with advertising – which is communication in bought space – but, of course, there is a catch.) It takes time, and in the accountancy profession time is certainly money; ask any client! Therefore in too many organizations PR is neglected, staff are busy, even overstretched, and opportunities are missed. Yet if the power of PR is consistently ignored then at worst not only are opportunities missed but the image that occurs by default may actually damage your business prospects.

In many ways, therefore, time spent on PR is time well spent and often more a case of relationships rather than resources.

Press Relations

This very specific form of PR can pay dividends, though you must bear in mind that, unlike an advertisement you can not guarantee what is going to be said. Having said that, there is no reason of course to feel that the press will be critical.

Where then do you start? There are routine mentions and more particular stories, and in part much of the impact of both sorts of material is cumulative. Clients will sometimes comment on this: 'we seem to see mentions of the firm pretty regularly', but have difficulty remembering the exact context of what was said or more likely written. To achieve this cumulative impact you need to be constantly on the lookout for opportunities of mention.

Even routine matters, perhaps the appointment of a new partner or a move of office, may be written up. All that is necessary is first to remember to make these announcements, and then to take a disproportionate amount of care and attention as to how they are made. For instance, the announcement of an appointment is much more likely to be printed if there is a photograph with it. This takes a little more organizing but is well worth the trouble. So the first necessity is to be able to issue an appropriate, acceptable press release. Figure 3 sets out the key principles and provides an example.

Beyond the routine announcement things get a little more difficult. News means exactly that, and, while it may be of interest to you that the firm has 25 partners, inhabits an eighteenth century mansion, or specializes in tax problems for rich landowners, a journalist will tend to find it difficult to imagine readers starry-eyed with excitement as they read it in his newspaper or journal. You will have to find something with more of an element of news to it; it may be genuinely different, it may be a first comment on something but it must truly have something of genuine interest about it.

If you become known as a source of good comment, stories and articles, then your press contacts will start to come to you and the whole process may gain continuity and momentum.

Composing a Press Release

There are two, perhaps conflicting, aspects to putting together a Press Release that will stand a good chance of publication. The first is to comply with the 'form' demanded by the newspapers, magazines and journals to whom you send your release; the second is to stand out as being of genuine interest from the very large number of releases received.

Take the 'form' first:

- • It should carry the words 'Press (or News) Release' at the top, together with the date, preferably at the top left hand side of the first page.
- If an embargo is necessary, (ie, a request not to publish before a certain date, to ensure news appears as near as possible simultaneously – once an item has been in print others will consider it of less interest) it should be clearly stated 'EMBARGO: not to be published before (time) on (date)'. Underline or use capitals for emphasis.

Figure 3 Composing a Press Release

- Also at the top you need a heading, not too long but long enough to indicate clearly the contents of the release or to generate interest in it.
- Space it out well, wide margins, reasonable gaps between paragraphs and so on. This allows sub-editors to make notes on it.
- If it runs to more than one page make sure it says 'continued' or similar at the foot of the page, even break a sentence at the end of the page.
- Similarly, to make it absolutely clear that there is no more many put 'end' at the foot of the last page.
- Use newspaper style. Short paragraphs. Short sentences. Two short words rather than one long one.
- Keep it brief, long enough to put over the message and onto a second page if necessary, but no more.
- The first sentences are crucial and need to summarize as far as possible the total message.
- Avoid overt 'plugging' (although that may well be what you are doing). Do not mention names etc right at the beginning, for example.
- Try to stick to facts rather than opinions: '...this event is being arranged for all those interested in minimizing their tax liability' is better than '...this event will be of great interest to all those wanting to minimize their tax liaibility'.
- Opinions can be given, in quotes, and ascribed as such to an individual. This works well and can be linked to the attachment of a photograph (which should be a black and white print and clearly labelled in case it gets separated from the release).
- Do not overdo the use of adjectives, it can jeopardize credibility.
- Avoid underlining things in the text (this is used as an instruction in printing to put words underlined in italics).
- Separate notes to the journal from the text as footnotes, for example, 'photographers will be welcome'; they could get printed as part of the story.
- Never omit from a release, at the end, a clear indication of from whom further information can be sought and their telephone number (even if this is on the heading the first page).

Figure 3   Composing a Press Release (contd)

- Make sure finally that it is neat, well typed and presentable and that it lists enclosures. Obvious perhaps, but important.

Figure 3   Composing a Press Release (contd)

1 May 1987

Practical Guidance for the Accountant on the Gentle Art of Persuasion – a new Publication from Kogan Page

As the relaxation of restriction on accountants promotional activity continues, Kogan Page today published 'The Accountant's Guide to Practice Promotion', a comprehensive review which describes a practical, systematic approach to the promotion of the practice.

It reviews both the process of putting together a promotional plan and comments on its implementation. It has sections covering the various techniques involved including advertising, public relations and presentation skills. The book has been written by Patrick Forsyth, a Director of marketing and training consultants, Marketing Improvements Limited, who conducts courses on marketing topics for the Institute of Chartered Accountants. The author commented:

> 'Promotional, presentational and sales techniques have not traditionally been regarded as the Accountant's stock-in-trade. But, in a profession where many have felt that "nice guys don't sell",... competitive pressures are changing the situation and many are having to get to grips with these techniques. The book is designed specifically to help this process.'

The book shows how a practice can be persuasively presented, yet in a way that maintains the professionalism of the business and is acceptable, indeed, useful to clients.

The book is available now, and can be obtained from Kogan Page Ltd, 120 Pentonville Road, London N1 at a cost of £12.95 (+10% p&p)   ENCLOSED

photograph of the author

for further information please contact: Jenny Ertle
Kogan Page Ltd
120 Pentonville Road
London N1
Telephone 01-278 0433

Speaking Assignments

'By their deeds ye shall know them', but with any service it is not that simple. The client must take your competence to carry out any particular project on trust, or rather he will make inferences, looking at something he can see or measure and likes and literally says to himself 'that means they should be able to perform what I want well'.

Formal presentations, whether at functions you have convened or events at which you have been invited to speak, provide a dramatic example of this principle. They can be a way both of developing the overall image of the firm and prompting specific enquiries. Taking advantage of this potential opportunity area is dependent on cultivating opportunities to speak and on the firm being able to field people who can do a good job on such an occasion.

There is all the difference in the world between being willing to speak, and being invited. There are countless opportunities, at conferences, seminars, association meetings and so on. All have hard pressed organizers who often find it difficult to find the right people to speak. Keep in touch with them. They look in turn to others, for example the secretary of a trade association, to recommend speakers to them. Keep in touch with these people too.

Local radio too, with an expanding network of both commercial and BBC stations, presents regular opportunities, though it is wise to brief yourself on how an interview is carried out before appearing for the first time.

The important point to remember is that if you, or one of your colleagues, does undertake a speaking assignment, you (or he) must do it well enough. How well is that? In promotional terms it means well enough to make an impact that will effect image and prompt enquiries, ultimately well enough to be asked back. That way the process becomes less time-consuming and more effective. What is more, as some speaking engagements pay a fee, it can even provide promotion that pays.

Finally, do not neglect the audience you have among your own clients. The kind of function you perhaps run at Christmas which is primarily social may benefit from a short, but more formal, presentation. Other occasions, for example a post budget briefing, certainly demand a crisp, competent presentation.

How to Make an Effective Presentation

'The human brain', as a wise man once said 'is a wonderful thing. It starts working the day you are born, goes on and on and only stops the day you get up to speak in public'. In fact, even an inexperienced speaker can give a clear, interesting presentation and hold an audience's attention, it is only a question of learning the necessary skills.

And now, how can you make sure it stands out? Fewer rules exist here, but there are perhaps two:

- Do not 'cry wolf'. Save releases for when you really have a story. If you send a series of contrived ones there is a danger that a good one will be ignored among them.
- Make sure the story sounds interesting and, without overdoing things, be enthusiastic about it. If you are not, why would they be? Perhaps the only good thing in the world that is contagious is enthusiasm.

Finally, an example, included with some caution because a good Press Release thrives on an element of individuality. While it may illustrate some of the points mentioned above it should not be copied slavishly.

Overall there are three key factors involved if a presentation is to be well received. First, it must be audible. This seems obvious, but if people have difficulty hearing they will not take in even the best turned phrase or way of putting things. Secondly, it must be understandable. If people have difficulty following the sense they will not keep up or find the presentation easy. Thirdly, it should be enjoyable to listen to, perhaps the most important factor of all and one that is dependent very largely on the confidence of the speaker. What creates confidence? Well, for one thing, the security of preparation.

Preparation

This is quite simply the key to success. Carefully selected and prepared material will be more likely to go over well, and familiarity with the material gives a sound foundation to your confidence. Preparation should consider:

The kind of audience to whom you must speak: consider carefully who they are, how much they already know about your topic, their attitude to it and how fast they can take in more. Clearly if you anticipate hostility or great interest, you can pitch your presentation accordingly. Unless the presentation is directed accurately at the audience there is a danger they will quickly feel bored.

The purpose of your talk: the objective will condition the whole nature of the talk, for example is it intended to give a broad overview or detailed information? Do you want the audience to do anything as a result of what you say? Whatever the objective, the talk must reflect it in its nature and form. With the audience and objective clearly in mind you can proceed to the next stage.

Writing down what you will say: remember that all good presentations must have a beginning, a middle and an end, so it is a good idea to jot ideas down under these headings. Often there is more material than you need for the time allotted so ideas have to be pruned, put into the most logical sequence and key points, or even sentences, noted. Most effective speakers do not read their notes, (it is in fact very difficult to produce a fluent talk that way), indeed a full text may often be avoided so that this cannot happen. Notes should therefore highlight key points, headings, examples and so on with only perhaps the first and last sentence written out in full. Cards may be better than sheets, but whichever method you use they should be numbered – the accident of dropping unnumbered pages just before a talk is guaranteed not to be good for confidence. A good tip is to number them in reverse, ie the last page is 1, thus you can always see clearly how many more there are to cover, which is useful in judging when you will finish.

Format of Speaking Notes

The format of any notes from which you speak is important. Their form may well have a bearing on how well the presentation goes. Some speakers (but relatively few), can manage without notes; others use a few headings and others still need something more elaborate.

By way of example, consider something down the middle. Figure 4 is the opening of a talk on Marketing Accountancy (a conference paper I presented, reported, as near as I can rcall, verbatim). It also shows the kind of note that might well be suitable as 'speaker's notes' for this. Two colours used on this would give added guidance.

It is very much a matter of personal preference and

experience how this is done, but worth a conscious effort to find the format that suits you best. The overall presentation planning chart (Figure 5) will help plan the structure ans content of any talk.

With practise you will get to know how many minutes your chosen style of notes represents.

Ladies and Gentlemen, Good Morning

I am very conscious of being the only non-accountant here. Your conference programme is full of important topics, concerned mainly with the constant updating that must go on continuously in a profession that is, I know, so dependent on being able to guide its clients through a jungle of constantly changing technicalities.

My talk appears under the title 'Indecent Exposure? – a promotional plan for the practice'. This too is an important topic, but one that many in the profession view with mixed feelings. I will try to bear this attitude in mind as I speak.

Though it is an attitude which reminds me of the story of the businessman who didn't believe in promotion or advertising and didn't do any – until he had to put a 'For Sale' notice outside his premises!

So it is with accountancy and promotion, something has to generate sufficient business and the question is therefore not so much whether you need promotion but how much is needed. Given that you want to run a profitable practice, to receive more in fees than you incur in costs, and to increase business – then the need for a process that ensures a sufficient flow of work is not in doubt. Promotion is concerned with producing that flow of business, how much is necessary is dependent on the market; so is what manner of promotion is best, though this is influenced also by the ethical rules of the profession.

Some of these ethical rules, like the precise circumstances in which you can distribute a brochure, and which seem to an outsider a little bit like 'Alice in Wonderland', are under review. More of that later.

It is certain that competitive pressures have increased and that in a profession convinced that 'nice guys don't sell' there has nevertheless been a gradual acceptance of the need for marketing – this process continues steadily if suspiciously.

Figure 4

And what about this word Marketing. It is in no sense a magic formula. Currently perhaps there is still a situation where too many accountants don't even understand the word. Not surprisingly perhaps as it is confusingly used.

Marketing is not advertising (the focus of much, perhaps too much, of the ethical debate) nor is marketing a euphemism for selling. The word is used in three main ways. Let me try to make these clear. First, it is a *concept*, that of seeing our business through the eyes of the customer or client and ensuring profitability through providing value satisfaction to him. Secondly, it is a *function*, the total management process that coordinates this approach, anticipating the demands of clients, identifying and satisfying those needs by providing the right service at the right price and time, and in the right place and manner. Thirdly, it describes a series of *techniques* that make the process possible. These include research, advertising, selling and other promotional factors and involve many other considerations from how we set prices to the image we want to project.

Everything implied by all three is important to accountancy and can play a part in developing the practice.

The other factor to have clear is our minds is the way in which the pressures of competition are increasing. Not so much business just walks in the door these days, and the role competition plays in this trend can, I think, be divided into three areas of influence.

These are professional competition, particularly the activity of the larger firms, 'unprofessional' competition, that of banks and others, and the clients themselves, ever demanding greater value for money.

Let's look at these in turn ...'

(And so on – this is the first few minutes of an hour's talk).

Figure 4 (contd)

Conference Notes

Ladies and gentlemen

only non-accountant — other topics
↓
constant updating process

(title) INDECENT EXPOSURE — a promotional plan for practice
↓
*also important topic, viewed
with mixed feelings.*

story of man who did not believe in ad (For Sale)

So it is with accountancy — not whether promotion is necessary but how much

Promotion → profit growth

influenced by market and ethics

competitive pressures (nice guys don't sell) →

acceptance of marketing — confusing
↓
definition (not advertising

*used in 3 ways — concept
— function
— techniques — all apply*

(Next) competitive pressures — (not so much walks in the door)

again 3 elements

↓ *professional*

unprofessional

client pressure

Figure 4 (contd)

Beginning

POINT 1
1. Value to audience?
2. Evidence?
3. Attention?
4. Objections?
5. Agreement?

Middle

1. Attention?
2. Rapport?
3. Theme?
4. Structure?
5. Summary of needs?

POINT 2
1. Value to audience?
2. Evidence?
3. Attention?
4. Objections?
5. Agreement?

POINT 3
1. Value to audience?
2. Evidence?
3. Attention?
4. Objections?
5. Agreement?

1. Theme?
2. Summary of points?
3. Commitment

End

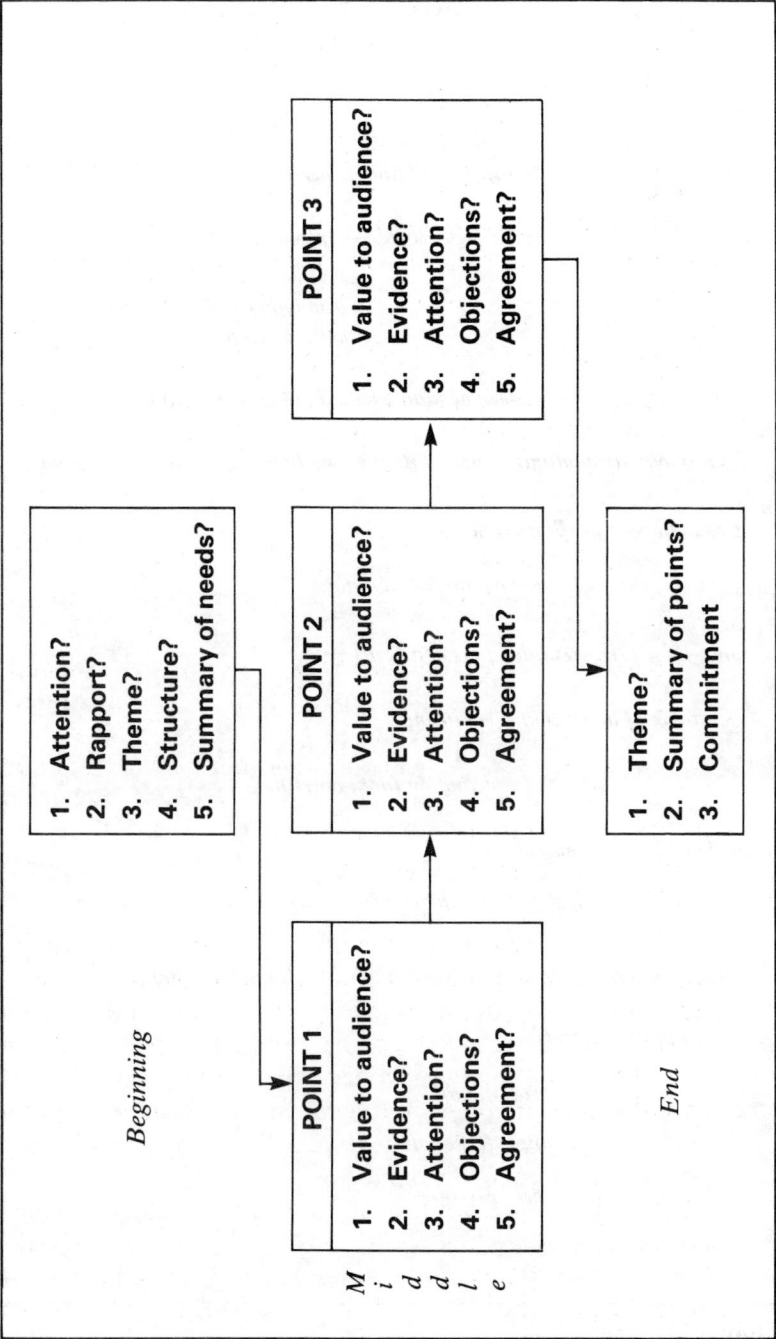

Figure 5 Presentation Planning Chart

Giving the Presentation

A number of points are important once you get to your feet:

Words: some people have a natural feel for language, others must work at it; observation and practise can help. Other factors, for example, repetition, can add to what you say; as can, comparisons, contrasts, aliteration, and anything that adds a descriptive element to what is said. But it is the *way* you use the words that is even more important.

Voice: whether or not you have a naturally attractive voice you can add to it's effectiveness by the way you use it. Start with an appreciation of how you come across now. This is easily done with a small tape recorder. Then you can work on:

* speed – not so fast that your speech is garbled or glib, and not so slow that it is boring.
* pace – the ebb and flow of talk adds variety and spontaneity.
* pitch – this can change the feeling; for example, putting a question mark into a phrase. Some women may need to pitch their voices down a little to avoid coming over 'squeaky'.
* pauses – these can change the sense of what is said and add impact. A pause can be very effective ... even dramatic ... if used in the right place.
* emphasis – this probably needs exaggerating from normal speech and is important not only to sense, but can add interest, enthusiasm or urgency to a message.

All of these together, with the overall tone of authority or friendliness for instance, can be used to add to the delivery.

Visual aids: these can add to any presentation and perhaps the most important is yourself. Stand up, match your expression to your words, use your hands to emphasize points and avoid visual factors that distract such as mannerisms (tapping your pen, rattling the loose change in your pocket, shuffling notes, looking at your watch). If you want to keep an eye on the time put your watch flat on the table or lectern in front of you where your audience cannot see you glance at it.

Other visual aids should be used as appropriate; too many can become confusing, and they must be allowed to speak for themselves. If, for example, you put a graph of some sort on an overhead projector slide, then pause for a moment so that people can take it in – they will not read and listen at the same time. Finally, once you have used a visual aid and passed on, remove it, switch off the projector or remove or cover a flipchart so that it does not distract; and remember 'a picture is worth a thousand words' – checklists are useful but a sufficient proportion of your visual aids should be visual.

Timekeeping: this is an important discipline. The audience should know how long you will speak (this means you tell them if the Chairman does not) and then stick to what you have said. If you overrun acknowledge the fact, saying perhaps that you must close in a couple of minutes but would like to add a couple of points first. Not only is all this a courtesy to your audience but it prevents the group having a part of their minds busy wondering when you are going to stop!

A good structure to the talk is essential. This will include an attention-getting start and clear instructions, a logically organized main theme developed in the middle of the presentation, and an ending that wraps up the topic and, if possible, finishes with a flourish. Figure 5 illustrates this shape in more detail. Putting a point over with confidence and enthusiasm can give you the impact you want. Approached in this way, while you may still be nervous (even the best, most experienced speakers are), there will be no need to be worried. This is certainly a skill more and more accountants must be comfortable with; in many of the larger firms it is a subject of priority in training, and it is an ability that clients respect and may increasingly demand.

Centres of Influence

This phrase is used to describe a group that perhaps consists of a number of different kinds of organization, having in common their ability to recommend, introduce or even just produce opportunities for meeting people. They range from national bodies, for example, associations, to social groups, trade bodies, individuals such as the local bank manager or solicitor and even charities. Some imply only the need to keep in touch, though this must be done systematically, that is, regularly and acceptably. The latter implies a maximum frequency of contact which must be judged in each case, but acceptability is also conditioned by manner and the *reason* a contact is made. It will make a greater impact if there is a particular reason, even a superficial one for the contact. Others need a more active involvement, like being on the committee or even Chairman (or Treasurer?) of a relevant association or similarly run body.

In either case time is spent and there is the danger both that, because it is time consuming, nothing happens and at the other extreme that someone gets so sucked into committee work other priorities suffer. Yet such activity is clearly a cost-effective way of producing leads.

So, perhaps the best way of handling this area is to ensure a consciously organized shareout of activity, with different partners taking on different 'centres' with whom they maintain contact. This way the load is spread. If, in addition, a regular reporting back occurs and this is in turn linked to a record noting where new business emanates from, then it is comparatively easy to make sure such effort is cost-effective and a real return is in evidence.

In many a practice it is an area where prevailing wisdom is often misinformed or out-of-date. For example, a bank manager one partner regularly lunches every few months may produce nothing, while another who is beginning to pass on prospective clients is neglected.

This is another area that should not be allowed to go by default and it pays to ascertain all the 'centres' worth dealing with, list in order of priority the most important, spread the responsibility around and monitor results. This may mean leaving some out. So be it. Priorities can always be changed and there is no reason for the list to remain static.

Articles/papers

While even a simple press release is dependent on having something to say, this is even more true of articles. Their promotional power is often considerable and they can sometimes earn a small fee. More importantly, they provide an opportunity to demonstrate approach, expertise, competence and professionalism; accountancy is a service business where the 'product' cannot be tried and tested, therefore as a form of exposure to the public they are especially valuable. (Why else would I agree to write this book!)

Investigation will often show a much greater list of potential places of publication than first thought might suggest, and many periodicals find it quite difficult to find people to contribute – or at least to do so reliably. Those you may deal with on journals like to work with people who 'deliver'; that is who present a manuscript on time, tied to whatever layout and form the magazine specifies. Those who do this and write something worth publishing can expect to be asked to contribute again or may make further suggestions themselves.

The important thing is that opportunities in this area are taken up. If the senior partner cannot string one word in front of the other, then someone else can do it. One person may brief another to do the writing (joint authorship is quite acceptable). It is worth organizing, planning and thinking about in these ways so that something happens – the daunting thought of a blank sheet of paper and 2000 words to write will otherwise tend to ensure that nothing does happen.

Conclusion

A number of times in this chapter I have used the words 'it does not just happen', and certainly at this stage of summing up, I make no apology for using them again – planning promotional activity is the key to success in this whole area and it does not just happen. The previous chapter sets out the sequence and thinking process involved. There is a danger that this seems a daunting process and thus gets left undone, with any promotional tasks being handled on an *ad hoc* basis. Although an element of promotion can usefully become responsive, for instance a request for a specific article which is then written, unless the firm is to be at the mercy of events there is no escape from the need to plan.

In fact, the planning process need not be onerous, certainly not once the first plan which may be a more complicated process has been set out. This is because planning is a 'rolling' process, the plan needing updating and extending once it exists rather than starting again from scratch. As long as it exists in writing, this updating need not be elaborate. The key element is probably best kept in diary form, translating overall intentions to timed action and this can be run forward literally month by month.

Another crucial factor in the whole process is responsibility. It is in many ways not easy for a partnership, geared to directing the professional work, to ensure that other tasks, however important, get the necessary commitment; expecially one that may in the early stages be considered peripheral. Responsibility means just that, it does not imply doing all the work, but making sure it does get done. Someone has to take on this role. In the larger firms it is easier. As I write this, I have just had a conversation with someone in one large firm, who, when asked his job title said 'Director of Marketing'.

This, it transpired, was a full time role, a new post and the result of recruitment outside the firm. This is not to say everyone must follow the same route, but in terms of commitment to marketing it is a sign of the times. At the other end of the scale, examples of current practice, such as were mentioned in the introduction, like separate sales review meetings, are very much a step in the right direction.

A further key to success in promotion is coordination, and with that, timing. Whether it is making sure the graduate recruitment brochure is ready *before* the recruitment campaign starts or that sales activity is implemented at the right stage of the financial year, both are critical. It is in this respect that the laying of responsibility is so important as someone must set the timing and pull the strings together – something it is difficult to achieve through a committee.

If one accepts that the process discussed here is necessary and even assuming the process is well coordinated, then the detailed skills involved may still be to one degree or another alien. This in turn may imply the necessity for either external support or training or both. The courses the Institute now presents on sales and marketing topics go some way in providing help but with some large firms spending considerable resources on training, more than this may be helpful. Certainly in circumstances where, for instance, a new brochure is being put together, it is a pity to 'spoil the ship for a "ha'porth of tar"'. A graphically superb treatment of a poor message in a brochure may do just that and might have benefitted from a slightly greater measure of professional assistance to make sure it was right.

The last point which should be made in summary concerns commitment and persistance; this applies both overall and to the finer details. It is often that extra call, sometimes not made, to an editor about a possible article, to an intermediary about a possible collaboration that pays dividends. It is easy to rationalize, usually with reference to the pressures (and fees) of client work, as to why there is never time to follow up opportunities. On the other hand, it is galling to follow one up and find that you have been pipped at the post by a competitor.

Of course it is easier to read about the promotional ideas and planned approaches presented here than it is to implement them, and just saying 'yes, we should do that' does not take you too far. Therefore to bridge the gap between the theory and implementation the need to originate and implement a promotional plan should again be stressed. The approach to planning is essentially practical, and is designed to facilitate implementation and increase the chances of gaining new business.

After that it is up to you. An increasing proportion of the business and profit you want in the future will be dependent on promotion.

Promotion has only one final objective, to produce more business. To do that it must be persuasive; promotion that is so circumspect as to be less than persuasive is not just less effective but useless. This is as true of direct mail as of anything yet discussed. This is the subject of the next chapter.

Chapter 5

Direct Mail

**'Someone somewhere is waiting
for a letter from you'**

This specialist technique is given a perhaps disproportionate amount of space for a number of reasons. It is, in the UK at least, a recent addition to permitted techniques. It is less straightforward than might appear. Many of the principles explored in detail here have relevance for other forms of promotion, a brochure for example may or may not be designed for mailing purposes but is always important.

Like all promotional techniques, direct mail cannot be considered in isolation. It is part of the mix, and may most appropriately be used in conjunction with other techniques, all intended to produce enquiries that will then need to be converted, by personal persuasive selling skills, to actual signed-up clients.

So not only is there now an extra technique to get to grips with, but a very particular one, and potentially a very useful one. Yet feelings about direct mail seem to run high. Some people regard it as intrusive. Everyone appears to know someone who has been mailed three times in the same week about something entirely inappropriate, and addressed wrongly, as 'Dear Madam'. Some people regard it as more than intrusive, ranking it either with picking your teeth in public or being unkind to small, inoffensive furry creatures.

In the accountancy world, and elsewhere, existing views may be deeply ingrained. Way back in the days BA (Before Advertising) whether such views were accurate or not, did not matter, no advertising was permitted and there the matter ended. Now, after the changes to the guidelines that allowed advertising, and the recent amendments that added direct mail to the list of permissible techniques a whole range of elements are available and make up the promotional mix. They must all be viewed dispassionately and the best mix selected and deployed. 'Best' in this context means most cost-effective, most likely to have the desired, promotional effect. If one element is omitted or underrated simply through prejudice, that is a waste.

Business is becoming too precious to allow any to go by default.

Direct mail is in fact only a form of advertising. No more, no less, albeit a specialized form. It is used very successfully in a wide range of industries and applications, many of them perfectly respectable – Charities, Banks, Building Societies and so on. What is more, although of course there is the occasional annoyance, it is used for the most part without upsetting the people to whom it is directed. If they are not interested, they throw it away; a process not really so unlike turning over an advertisement page in a magazine in which one is not interested. Of course direct mail is wasteful. It hurts to think of so many of your carefully penned words going in the bin. But it is no more wasteful than other forms of advertising. All advertising is in a sense wasteful – what matters is whether it produces a cost-effective response, whether it pays for itself long term.

Contrary to popular belief, direct mail *is* read. The Post Office who spend a great deal of time and money studying the effectiveness of direct mail, recently demonstrated through research that more than 90 per cent of it is opened and more than 75 per cent of it is read. The trick is less to achieve this therefore, than to ensure your offering will stand out from others, will generate interest and will be seen as persuasive.

So direct mail does not replace anything, it adds to the range of techniques available. It is no more a magic formula than any other individual technique. But it is likely to suit accountancy well. It is flexible; certainly more flexible than advertising. Direct mail may mean either four letters, 40, 400, 4000 or 40,000. It does not have to be done on the grand scale, it can be targetted at small specific groups; it can be undertaken progressively with so many shots per week or month being sent. It is personal and can be directed at the decision makers, their advisers or both. It is controllable, can be tested, implemented progressively and results can be monitored to ensure it provides a cost-effective element in the total promotional mix. As it is likely to be low cost per contract, and campaigns can be varied so much in size, there are likely to be few practices which could not experiment with the technique. It is specific and may be directed broadly, selling the firm, or be part of the promotion of particular services.

Furthermore, direct mail has a lot going for it. It is a proven technique in other fields, it can be used on a small scale, it can be targeted on specific market segments, and it can be tested and monitored much more easily than many other forms of promotion. It may well prove even more important to practice development than other forms of advertising. Time will tell.

So, if you have read this far, I hope you continue with an open mind to a review of exactly what direct mail is and how it can contribute to your overall promotional activity.

Consider first some of the background factors and the basics of the component parts of a direct mail campaign before looking at how creatively, the response to it can be ensured.

Who to Mail

Who, rather than what, because it is very much better to mail individuals by name rather than organizations. It is of course possible to address 'The Finance Director, XYZ Limited' but if you know the name of the appropriate contact this will always product better results.

The intention is to communicate with decision makers, and to a lesser extent, with influencers. However, the people an accountancy firm needs to approach are not an easy group to define. It will vary depending on the size of the firm, where it is located and what mixture of services it offers. It will include individuals, owner managers of small businesses, Managing Directors, Finance Directors and internal accountants. And it will include Bank Managers, Solicitors, and those in insurance and others who can in any way act as recommenders.

Often in fact, accountants do not have a clear idea of who is most important. A firm may think they are in touch with all local Bank Managers, while having no system to check that contact is occurring regularly, nor to link results to the contacts which do occur. No system may exist either to hold names and addresses in comprehensive form so that they can be mailed conveniently. As a result contact may be diluted with an important influencer. There may be similar uncertainty regarding client contacting, and certainly with prospective clients.

An interesting area for research, one that is being used by some, is into exactly how, by whom and in what circumstances accounting services are purchased.

The effectiveness of any mailing is clearly dependent on mailing the right people, ie, on the quality of the mailing list. There are two separate approaches to the question of lists, either build your own or use other peoples (or both as they are not mutually exclusive).

Outside sources of lists abound, available most often for rent, sometimes for outright purchase. Rented lists are well guarded and will always include 'seeded' names so that the owner of the list can monitor their use. This prevents lists hired for one time use being copied and used again. Using outside lists can be very useful, not least because it avoids the problem of holding them, printing off labels and much of the administrative detail involved. Sources of lists are well documented (the regularly updated 'Direct Mail Databook' published by Gower Publishing is a good reference).

At the same time informal sources ranging from companies you know to Chambers of Trade or Commerce may also be useful. In addition you can cull names from a wealth of directories (those that do not make their entries available in list form) not simply to mail once, but to record and use again.

Holding and Maintaining the List
Mailing lists are a perishable commodity. They have to be maintained and updated. The latter is important; people move jobs, positions, addresses and like to be addressed correctly.

The simplest form of list maintenance is a card index and for some small purposes this may be quite adequate. Beyond this some settle for lists on A4 sheets that can be photocopied direct onto A4 labelled sheets. Beyond this the computer revolution has made many a labelling system obsolete. Although some firms still use metal plate systems for example, for all practical purposes list holding now necessitates a computer. As a result most, even quite small, systems are able to hold lists and can be programmed with additional facilities (for instance, mail-merging systems which allow letters to be produced with the name on the label used in the letter).

Computer companies, and their distributors, will be only too willing to offer help and advice. If you have an existing system the new element must be compatible with it and while there is a profusion of good standard software available it is important that this will give you the exact operation you want.

For example, you may wish to:
— print out by company/organization as well as individual names
— rebate-sort, ie to deliver post to the Post Office presorted in a way that qualifies for lower rates (though note that it also takes longer to deliver)

— link into other record systems, client, debtors etc.
— print quietly or at a certain speed
or simply avoid your labels looking as if they have come off a computer system.

All the caveats of purchasing this sort of equipment apply. Like all such systems, exactly what will suit you needs some investigation if you are to end up with something truly suitable. Even when you do, then as the saying has it 'when your system works well, it's obsolete'; I make no attempt here to itemize specific equipment or software as what is available changes as you watch. But this is no excuse not to make decisions to buy. However long you wait, there will always be a better system available tomorrow.

Deciding the Message

Before any sort of mailshot or campaign can be put together, you must decide the objectives; what are you selling and what response are you looking to prompt? You may say that the answer to this is obvious. You want to sell the firm and its services and you want people to buy them, but this may prove too simplistic a view to enable the construction of an effective mailshot.

Like all promotion, direct mail can only produce enquiries. It may do so in specific ways:

— requests for information
— agreement to a meeting
— acceptance of an invitation to a function

for example, but recipients are unlikely to come, cheque in hand, to the door saying 'Please take this, and start Monday'. So you will have to sell them on a route to a purchase decision as well as on the service you offer.

To do this, you must be clear what the service is. If you ask (I do – on courses) an accountant to describe his firm and the services it provides, he will usually do so by saying they offer such things as 'personal service', 'a comprehensive range of accounting services', or 'partner supervision of every client's work'. This sounds fine until you ponder, or ask, what exactly is 'personal service', for instance, – service by people? So? It is not exactly a full description. This problem is compounded by the fact that if you ask another accountant the same question he says such things as 'We offer personal service ... a comprehensive range of services ... partner supervision of every client's work.'

The rather introspective attitude that will often produce this line, is unlikely to excite the prospective client; it will now even make it easy for him to differentiate one firm from another. In circumstances where so many accountants report that it is now the norm for a prospective client to talk to more than one accountant, it is clearly important that some differentiation should be built into the message.

Until this area is sorted you stand little chance of putting together an effective direct mail campaign. Two approaches will clarify the situation. The first relates to the business plan for the practice. It is here that the base message as to what kind of firm you are, and want to be, is forged. It may be a long and difficult process, but there needs to be a consensus as to the 'positioning' for the firm. Is it really to be all things to all people, or does it specialize in some way, in which case in what way? This is not to say such statements are unchangeable, and are cast in tablets of stone. The firm is no doubt evolving, the market is certainly dynamic, so what is right for today will have to include a direction for tomorrow. Usually, much of the thinking has been going on, much of the information is there; you have only to make yourself put into words, what – in detail – you really mean by saying 'personal service' in your firm to see how much more there is to say.

The same applies to individual services as has been stated for the firm. You do audits. What exactly does that mean? Some may be the statutory minimum. Even so you can spell out something about *how* they are carried out. Others almost certainly involve more than the minimum work being done. For each category you can more specifically state what is involved.

Secondly, you must be able to take the clients' view in the way you put over the message. It is empathy with the client that removes the introspection referred to earlier, and which will need to be reflected throughout the task of putting together any sort of direct mail promotion. Knowing how and why clients view your services as they do is a pre-requisite to putting any promotional material together, especially material for direct mail, which may be distributed widely and contain elements that are retained by recipients or used regularly for some time as with an accompanying brochure.

The Clients' Viewpoint

It has been said in other fields of business 'Don't sell products – sell benefits.' The same principle applies to accountancy. This is a crucial concept and, if you have not read the section headed 'The Clients' Viewpoint' in Chapter 4 (page 58), it will be appropriate to return to it before reading on.

The Response

As was mentioned at the beginning of this section having clear objectives for promotion includes having a clear idea what response is looked for as a result of receipt of the 'shot'. Simply, what do you want people to *do* if they are interested.

One action, extensively used elsewhere, should be mentioned here first but only to make clear that it is specifically *excluded* by the Institute's current ethical guidelines. That is telephone follow up. It is not currently permitted to say in your letter 'I will telephone you in a few days...' and then take the initiative. The need is thus to offer other options of response which will appeal, and do so sufficiently to prompt the recipient to take the initiative.

The temptation is perhaps to go for simplicity– you ring us; or for what we want most – come and see us for a discussion. The more persuasive you feel your message is the stronger this temptation may be.

Yet the same principle of empathy must be applied. The response, or responses – many direct mailshots provide a choice – must be made attractive in client terms. Will they want to send for more information? If so how much should we give them (without solving the problem) and in what form; will they want to meet us? – if so who – senior partner or specialist; where – our offices, theirs, a neutral venue; alone or with others – their colleagues, or others interested ie, would they expect or like to attend an event. Even minor details are important. For example, they may be more likely to phone us if we pay for the call, or return a card if the postage is paid.

Once a clear view has been formed in these areas, the question of how much direct mail is necessary must be considered, before considering the elements that make up a direct mail promotion.

How Much Direct Mail is Necessary?

How long is a piece of string? Unless the question is defined, any answer will do. Assume the firm has a quantified and timed statement of its total required level of fees for the planning period, usually the fiscal year. It must also assess what proportion of total fees can be expected to come in automatically and therefore the balance which will require positive promotion.

This balance must then be examined against marketing strategies and broken down by service type, by marketing or industry sector, and by existing or new clients to give purpose and focus to the promotion.

The greatest opportunity for immediate increased fees normally lies in selling more of the range of our services to existing clients. With current clients, the true needs are more obvious, our credibility is higher, and the amount of time needed to sell the ideas will thus be smaller, as will the selling cost. You can estimate this, and see what more is necessary from new promotion. In both cases this must be linked to your ability to sell.

As far as possible, the balance of business required should also be divided up and assigned to partners and managers as new business sales targets. Because clients naturally prefer professionals who can sell, rather than professional salesmen, all partners and managers responsible for clients should have sales targets agreed, even though they will not necessarily be of equal magnitude.

The targets, of course, represent only the forecast, the objective to be achieved. To complete the sales plan, the activities to achieve targets must be specified also. To recap on a topic referred to in Chapter 2 on marketing planning, thus we must know:

(a) How many proposals need to be accepted (whether formal or informal)?
     ie *Total new business fees required*
     Average new business order size
(b) How many proposals need to be submitted?
     ie Number of proposals accepted X average conversion rate
(c) How many enquiries must be received?

(d) How many new clients must be secured?
In which markets?
With which services?

The intention of such precise specification is twofold. First, so that any tactical activity is positive and not simply responsive. Secondly, that by timing the activities we avoid the 'feast and famine' cycle of work, so characteristic of many service companies and ensure promotional activity is paced so that we can cope with any positive response. For most firms ten enquiries a week for a year are more useful than 500 all on one day. Decisions in this area are dependent on the collection of appropriate information and a degree of analysis.

Causal analysis will define what cause/effect relationship exists between promotional effort, contacts gained and contracts booked. This helps us decide on the most cost-effective use of promotional time and money. Lead time analysis – analysing the lead times between contact and proposal, and proposal and booking, is critical in deciding when sales effort must be stepped up, or when recruitment will be needed. It also has tactical use in signalling possible cash flow problems several months ahead. If you can form a view of the number of new contracts necessary, for example:

Work required next year	£350,000	
Average assignment size	7,000	50 clients
Historic existing:		
new client ratio	46:4	4 new clients
Booked: proposed ratio	1:2	8 new proposals or £56,000 proposed to 8 prospective clients
Enquiry: proposed ratio	3:2	12 new contacts
		(NB: NOT one per month. Most must be made early in the year).

Note: Our lead time analysis may tell us that these must be generated in the first six months, at which stage we are seeking five new contacts per month for January to June.

then the size of any necessary promotional campaign is put into perspective. Balanced with a view of budget and an idea of the promotional 'mix', the amount of direct mail necessary through the year can be estimated. This kind of analysis will never be exactly right, but perfection should not be made the enemy of the good – a reasonable estimate, which will no doubt get better over time, can act as a useful signpost.

With this in mind, it is time to consider what makes up a direct mail campaign.

The Elements of the 'Shot'

What goes out to the client is put together from essentially four elements, brochures or leaflets, a covering letter, a reply facility and, of course, an envelope. While the envelope is always necessary (I cannot see postcards being used, though they are, very successfully, by the travel trade) the other components can be varied. A 'shot' might consist only of a letter, or only of a brochure, or of a brochure that incorporates a reply coupon; or it might be more elaborate, a letter plus two or three brochures and a reply form and a return envelope. Clearly many permutations are possible. Together the package must carry the total message and that message must be sufficiently persuasive to prompt action from a number of recipients which will make the whole exercise cost-effective. The phrase mailshot, implies one such mailing, a campaign implies a number over time which may be about different elements of the services, separate except that they are clearly from the same source. Alternatively, shots may be closer and linked, virtually one message stretched across say two separate entities so that repetition reinforces its impact.

As the way things are done in some cases relate to more than one element or indeed to the package as a whole, the next sections look at the basic considerations regarding each element:

— the envelope
— brochures and leaflets
— the covering letter
— the reply device

The process of creatively putting the promotion together is examined separately later, revisiting some of the elements.

In every case a range of possible approaches, styles and details are identified. Any mailshot using them all would simply submerge in its own gimmicks and become self defeating. Each does have its place however, and carefully orchestrated various combinations can be very effective. It is perhaps important not to take a censorious line in considering them.

Of course there are dangers of inappropriate approaches with a professional service such as accountancy, but bear the client in mind and remember what one man finds pushy another finds persuasive. What matters ultimately is what causes a satisfactory response, nothing that does so in a way clients find acceptable should be overlooked. Remember also that the effect of many detailed factors involved throughout the package builds up, a number of points which individually seem of little significance may together increase the response rate noticeably. That said, let us start by taking a look at what the recipient sees first.

The Envelope
This must be serviceable, obvious but if there are a number of enclosures it must get them to their destination unscathed. Some feel quality directly effects response rates, believing that a white envelope is better than a manilla one. Like many of the possible permutations that are being reviewed this can be tested (see page 122). An 'if undelivered return to address' can be included. This may help to avoid waste, or prompt updates to the list by identifying when things are wrongly addressed.

Of course some recipients will not see this as their secretaries will open the mail. But some will, and some secretaries will clip an informative envelope to the contents before passing it on. So you may consider having the first part of the message printed on the envelope. The purpose of the envelope carrying such a message is not so much to help ensure they are opened, (research shows most are), it is to influence the frame of mind in which they are opened, aiming to generate some, albeit small, interest even at this early stage. If such a message is appropriate it may be complete in itself – 'Details enclosed of how to reduce your tax bill', questioning – 'Do you want to pay less tax?' or leave more to be explained by the contents – 'A way to save money … details inside'.

Other devices are possible. For example a window envelope may allow a glimpse of the contents, colour may add to the effect and reflect a corporate colour used inside. Important though the envelope may be it is what is inside that really generates the response. Post office regulations specify how much and what form of printing is allowed on the envelope.

Brochures and Leaflets
These may be items used elsewhere, brochures you give to bank managers, leaflets you display in reception. There is however no reason why such material should be suitable and you may need

to produce new material, tailored specifically to the job to be done.

In either case the brochure is unlikely to set out to tell people 'everything there is to know about the firm', rather it must prompt a desire for discussion. Too much information can even have the reverse effect. One hotel, sending direct mail to prompt conference business, found the number of visits to look at the hotel doubled when they replaced a short letter and glossy comprehensive brochure with a longer letter, no brochure and an invitation. This is of course a different area but, with no experience yet in accountancy that can be quoted, this sort of parallel seems worth noting.

The production of brochures generally is an area of increasing professionalism, and great care is needed in defining the objective, creating the right message and making sure the brochure looks good and reflects the image the firm intends to project. The days of the bland, general brochure, very similar to those of other firms, describing the chronological history of the firm and everything it does, and intended to be used for everything is rapidly passing. What is needed is the ability to match each objective in each particular area with something specifically designed for the particular job. This may mean separate brochures for recruitment and client usage. It may mean the 'corporate' brochure is a folder with separate inserts aimed at different target groups or different types of client, or it may mean a revised brochure every year, it may even mean a difference between the sort of brochure that is right to give a prospective client after a preliminary meeting and the sort suitable to present an intermediary, such as a bank manager. For direct mail purposes the brochure or leaflet concerned must be specific to the objective set for the particular promotion. Brochures may need to be reasonably self standing. They may after all get separated from the covering letter, but the total content – letter plus brochure – needs to hang together, to produce a complete and integrated message.

Overall what must be created is something that is accurately directed at a specific group, with a clear objective in mind, and – above all – that is persuasive. This may seem basic; promotional material is there to inform but it must do so persuasively. That is its prime purpose. The profession has had a tendency in the past to produce material that, while no doubt ethical, is so circumspect as to be largely ineffective. This does not mean moving to something that is inappropriately strident, (which might in any case be self-defeating) but it does mean a greater emphasis on client need and benefits (what services do for people, rather than what they are).

Essentially a less introspective approach, better designed to its purpose, is the rule. What does this mean?

- a front cover that has the name of the firm clearly shown, and/or that makes some offer of benefit. The reader must be clear, at a glance, why he should read on.
- leaflets are expensive, so you cannot afford to waste space. There is, or should be lots to say about the services you provide.
- it should make clear how a reader makes contact with the firm. This is, after all, the whole purpose of the communication.
- photographs, or any illustrations, should be clear, captioned if appropriate, and have some bearing on the content.
- above all the text must be truly orientated to the client, their views, their needs, and persuasively and attractively written.

More than one brochure may be necessary, and these may be different in nature. For example let us assume a brochure is being sent about personal tax planning, if the chosen response is to try to persuade people to attend an informal seminar as a first step to an individual meeting, then two brochures may be necessary. One about the service and another, probably smaller, about the event.

There are few rules to be observed about brochures, and those one might define are made to be broken. This is because they must be creatively constructed to reflect the image of the firm graphically, differentiate it from its competitors and aim their chosen message directly at the target group addressed.

The Covering Letter

Basics first. It must look right. It must be attractively laid out, grammatically correct, and well presented. In selling a professional service this is especially important, it gives the impression that it has originated in an efficient and reputable firm.

The letterhead itself is important to the image, up to date yet not 'over the top' is what should be aimed at; not easy.

Subjective judgements are involved. Ultimately it is a matter of opinion and in a partnership this can sometimes mean a safe compromise which may dilute impact. Consider too whether your standard letterhead is right for direct mail. Perhaps you should have something different. The illustration, using material from my own company shows how the impact can be varied by putting information at the top of the page, as with many standard letterheads, using a different top, or moving all letterhead information to the bottom of the page so that a headline alone shows at the top.

Marketing Improvements Limited

Ulster House,
17 Ulster Terrace,
Outer Circle Regents Park,
London NW1 4PJ

Telephone: 01-487 5811
Telex: 299723 MARIMP G

Member of the UK Management Association

Asia Pacific Office,
07−04 LKN Building,
135 Cecil Street,
Singapore 0106

Telephone: 2235737/8
Telex: RS33436

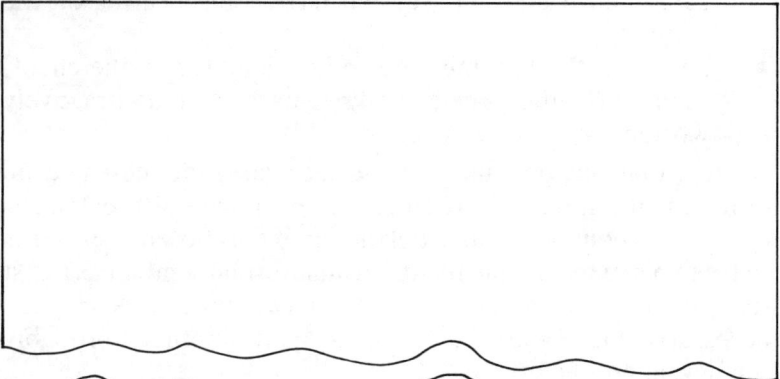

Directors: M.T. Wilson D.F. Wilson J.B.J. Lidstone D.I. Senton P.B. Kirkby R.A. Martin P. Forsyth D.M. Long
Associate Directors: S.C. Brayne D.A. Crane R.D. Murray T.W. Sealey
Registered Office: Ulster House, 17 Ulster Terrace, Outer Circle, Regents Park, London NW1 4PJ   Registered No. 800303 England.

**Marketing
Improvements Limited
Training Newsletter**

Ulster House,
17 Ulster Terrace,
Outer Circle Regents Park,
London NW1 4PJ

Telephone: 01-487 5811

Telex 299723 MARIMP G
Cables IMPMARK London NW1

European Office, 49 Avenue de l'Armee
1040 Brussels Telephone 733.47.39

The Salutation is important. Numbers may preclude individual salutations. If you are not saying 'Dear Mr Smith, or 'Dear John' what do you say? One answer is nothing. Simply start with a heading, it does not preclude your finishing with your name. In which case you should omit 'Yours sincerely' and set the name close enough to the text that it does not look as if the signature is forgotten, or matching the signature (or signatures even) in to give a personal touch. If you are only mailing small quantities you can actually sign them. Again the illustration (taken from a Marketing Improvements training course promotion) makes this clear.

The secrets of using
direct mail...

**Marketing
Improvements Limited
practical, proven, cost-effective training...**

It has highlighted many important aspects,
which I can now put into practice - an
excellent investment

We didn't say it, our clients did! In different ways and ...

Minimal time and cost spent on one of our courses can give you an
unfair   competitive advantage — don't hesitate to take it!

PATRICIA WELLINGTON   CORRINA HALL
CLIENT SERVICES EXECUTIVE   COURSE ADMINISTRATOR

Ulster House,
17 Ulster Terrace,
Outer Circle Regents Park,
London NW1 4PJ
Telephone: 01-487 5811
Telex: 299723 MARIMP G

Directors: M.T. Wilson, D.F. Wilson,
J.B.J. Lidstone, D.I. Senton,
P.B. Kirkby, R.A. Martin,
P. Forsyth, D.M. Laing.
Associate Directors: S.C. Brayne,
D.A. Crane, T.W. Sealey

Registered Office:
Ulster House,
17 Ulster Terrace,
Outer Circle Regents Park,
London NW1 4PJ
Registration No. 800303 England.

On other occasions a standardized opening is necessary, for example:

Dear Client (that at least is clear), Dear Sir, Dear Reader, Dear Colleague, Dear Taxpayer, Dear Finance Director (or other appropriate title) etc.

In many ways none of these is taken as more than a token greeting and, unless it is something really novel, has comparatively little impact. If you can find a form of words you like, perhaps almost anything is better than 'Dear Sir'!

In selling, face to face, you can adapt your approach to the individual you are with as the conversation proceeds. In a letter this is not possible, and a formula to structure the approach is useful. The classic sales acronym AIDA – Attention/Interest/Desire/Action works well in providing a structure for letters, and represents accurately the job to be done in prompting a response.

Before looking at how such a structure helps the composition of the letter, consider for a moment what happens when it is *received*. People seldom read a letter immediately in the same sequence in which it was written. Their eyes flick from the sender's address to the ending, then to the greeting and the first sentence, skim to the last – and then, if the sender is lucky, back to the first sentence for a more careful reading of the whole letter. Research has been done showing a clear sequence (see chart), so the first sentence is an important element in 'holding' the reader, and it should arouse immediate interest.

With that in mind consider the sequence of the letter, first as a whole. It will, I hope, be clear by now that the copy for the letter – as for the brochure(s) in fact – is crucial. You are unlikely to be able to dictate it, certainly not to begin with.

It will need thinking about, planning, and it will probably go through a number of drafts. Write down the key points, headings, identify the main benefits – create a skeleton. Then with some guidelines in mind you can look at how it all goes together.

Attention – the Opening

The most important part of the letter is the start. It will determine whether the rest of the letter is read. The opening may be quite short, a heading perhaps, a couple of sentences, two paragraphs, but it is disproportionately important. A good start will help as you write the letter as well as ensuring the

Letters: reading sequence

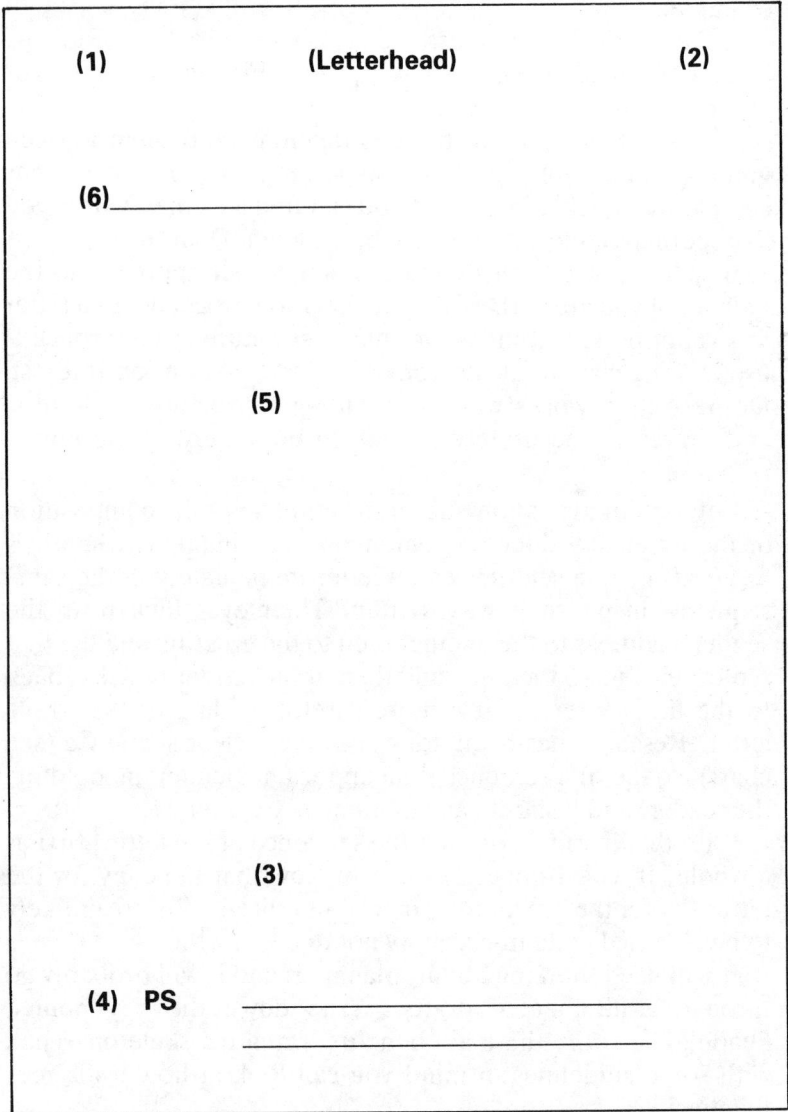

```
+--------------------------------------------------+
| (1)            (Letterhead)               (2)    |
|                                                  |
|                                                  |
|   (6)_____                           |
|                                                  |
|                                                  |
|                                                  |
|                (5)                               |
|                                                  |
|                                                  |
|                                                  |
|                                                  |
|                                                  |
|                                                  |
|                                                  |
|                (3)                               |
|                                                  |
|                                                  |
|   (4)  PS      _____          |
|                _____          |
+--------------------------------------------------+
```

(1), (2), (3)—information, taken in very fast. Who is it from?

(4)   — if there is one, the PS is the 'most read part of any letter'.

(5)   —an overall scan – do I have to read it all? – use of headings will affect this view.

(6)   —from beginning on (provided the opening is effective).

recipient reads it. Omit or keep references short and make subject headings to the point – the reader's point. Do not use 'Re'. Make sure the start of the letter will command attention – gain interest, and – lead easily into the main text. For example:

— ask a 'Yes' question.
— tell him why you are writing to him particularly.
— tell him why he should read the letter.
— flatter him (carefully).
— tell him what he might lose if he ignores the message.
— give him some 'mind bending' news (if you have any).

Interest/Desire – the Body of the Letter

The body of the letter runs straight on from the opening. It must consider the reader's needs or problems from his point of view. It must interest him. It must get the reader nodding in agreement – 'Yes, I wish you could help me on that'.

Of course you are able to help him. In drafting you must write what you intend for him and of course list the benefits, not features, and in particular benefits which will help him solve his problem and satisfy his needs.

You have to anticipate his possible objections to your proposition in order to select your strongest benefits and most convincing answers. If there is a need to counter objections, then you may need to make your letter longer and give proof, for example comment from a third party that benefits are genuine. However, remember to keep the letter as short as possible – but as long as necessary to complete the case. If that is two, three or more pages, so be it.

It is easy to find yourself quoting the literature that will accompany the letter to the reader. If you were writing a lecture on the subject, you would probably need all that information. When writing to a prospective client you have to select just the key benefits which will be of particular value to the reader and which support the literature.

The body copy must:
— keep the reader's immediate interest
— develop that interest with the best benefit
— win him over with a second and further benefits

The next job is to ensure action by a firm close.

Action – The Letter Ending

In closing you can make a (short) summary of the benefits of the proposition. Having decided on what action you are wanting the reader to take, you must be positive about getting it.

It is necessary to nudge the reader into action with a decisive close. Do not use:

'We look forward to hearing...'
'I trust you have given...'
'...favour of your instructions',
'...doing business with you',
'I hope I can be of further assistance',

which are really phrases added as padding between the last point and 'Yours sincerely', but real closing phrases, for example:

The alternative close
— ask him to telephone or write;
— telephone or use the reply-paid envelope;
— ask for a meeting or more information

Immediate gain
— return the card today and your profitability could be improved.

'Best' solution
— 'you want a system that can cope with occasional off-peak demands, that is easy to operate by semi-skilled staff and is presented in a form that will encourage line managers to use it.

The best fit with all these requirements is our system 'X'. Return the card indicating the best time to install it.'

Direct request
— post the card today
— telephone us without delay

In signing off do not automatically use 'Yours faithfully' for 'Dear Sir', and 'Yours sincerely' when the letter is addressed to an individual, but match to the tone of your general approach. Consider too who will have their name at the bottom. Replies will tend to come back to them, so should it be the senior partner, marketing partner, a tax specialist – and how well are they able to cope with any response? Make sure their name is typed as well, as signatures tend to be awkward to read, and that it includes a note of the position they hold in the firm. People like to know with whom they are dealing.

PS Remember the power of the postscript. Secretaries will

tell you they are for things inadvertently left out, direct mailers will tell you they get read. Use them for repetition or to add a final benefit – it can add strength to the message.
PPS Some people even use two!

Finally let us consider the language used in such letters. Many people have acquired a habit of artificiality in writing, approaching it quite differently from their way of talking to a client, and in a way that can lessen the danger of making a sale by overformality.

The Language
Remember your intention is to prompt the reader to action rather than demonstrate your 'Oxford English'. You should write much as you speak.

The following are some useful rules:

Be clear	—Make sure that the message is straightforward and uncluttered by 'padding'. Use short words and phrases. Avoid jargon.
Be natural	—Do not project yourself differently just because it is in writing.
Be positive	—In tone and emphasis (be helpful).
Be courteous	—Always
Be efficient	—Project the right image
Be personal	—Use 'I' – say what *you* will do.
Be appreciative	—Thank you is a good phrase

The checklist examines specific aspects of the language used in letters.

I hope this is not labouring the point. Accountants can have a tendency towards 'gobbledegook'. I recently saw a note tabled at a board meeting, recommendations proposed by the accountants about pension schemes. After a long silence someone said 'I don't understand it' immediately joined by a chorus of 'Neither do I'. The reasons, in some ways understandable, that allow this sort of thing to happen must not overlap into direct mail composition.

Persuasive language checklist
Avoid trite openings
We respectfully suggest...
We have pleasure in attaching...
Referring to the attached...
This letter is for the purpose of requesting...

Avoid pomposity
We beg to advise…
The position with regard to…
It will be appreciated that…
It is suggested that the reasons…
The undersigned/writer…
May we take this opportunity of…
Allow me to say in this intance…
Having regard to the fact that…
We should point out that…
Answering in the affirmative/negative…
We are not in a position to…
The opportunity is taken to mention…
Despatched under separate cover…

Avoid coldness and bad psychology
Advise/inform
Desire
Learn/note
Obtain
Regret
Trust

Avoid cliché endings
Thanking you in advance
Assuring you of our best attention at all times, we remain…
Trusting we may be favoured with…
Awaiting a favourable reply…
Please do not hesitate to…

Keep it simple – prefer short words to long
Approximately/about
Commencement/start
Elucidate/explain
Considerable/great

Prefer one or two words to several
at this moment in time/now
due to the fact that/because
in the not too distant future/soon
there can be no doubt about/it is certain
should the situation arise that/if

And short sentences.
Short paragraphs.
Aim for overall effect that sounds right read out loud. Try it. Get

a colleague to read your draft to you. Amend it. Sleep on it. Get it read again. There is no shame in taking a moment to get so important a piece of writing right.

Presentation
Finally remember that the end product should be neatly presented, in a way that the reader finds convenient.

To ensure the finishing touches and add impact you should for instance:

— Position the letter on the page according to the amount of the text. It is unattractive if there is a huge expanse of white below a very short letter. Position it lower down, in that case, or consider having two sizes of letterhead paper, and do short letters on the smaller sheets;
— 'Block' paragraphs, with double spacing between each paragraph for greater clarity and smartness;
— Leave at least 1½ inches at the foot of the page before going on to page two; leave a bigger space to avoid having only one or two lines (plus farewells) for the second page;
— Allow enough space for the signature, name and job title; rather carry the letter over on to another page than cram it in at the bottom;
— Note, at the foot of the last page, the enclosures mentioned in the text and sent with the letter;
— Staple the pages together to avoid losses;
— Number the pages;
— Number the paragraphs when a lot of points have to be covered;
— Underline all headings.

Remember layout of this sort of material cannot be simply left to the secretary or typist. How a letter is to be presented must be specified by the writer to prevent retyping.

Graphic emphasis can be made, in this word processor age, in a number of ways; with:

— CAPITALS
— underlining
—   indenting
— **bold type**
— colour
— *italics*

these, in whatever form and combination you select need specifying.

The Reply Device

This may be a coupon, a form to be completed, or self contained reply-paid card. Whatever format you select its use should be one hundred per cent clear. It is fatal to have someone interested to the point of taking action, then put off because how they take action seems unclear or complicated.

So make it clear. Decide what information you want. If you ask for a name and address, adding a request for their job title may make follow up just that little bit easier. Let them tick boxes rather than write essays. Let them send their business card rather than fill in anything.

Do not forget to include your telephone number, print it clearly and consider the freephone options. It is certainly a courtesy to use reply-paid letters or cards (or freepost). If you opt for reply-paid do make it first class, there is something incongruous about asking for an urgent response and then offering a second class envelope to send back.

Allow enough time, there are arrangements to be made, and you will need to liaise with the Post Office. The standard reply-paid format (below) seems straightforward, but requires a licence (thereafter you only pay for those that come back) and must conform to the prescribed format in terms of both size and style of printing.

Think carefully before you omit this element of the total package – an easy means of response can make all the difference to results. And do not treat it as a simple extra – check it carefully, particularly ask someone else if the description of *exactly* what you want done is clear, and the method of returning it simple and appropriate.

Reply-paid envelope – type size, quantity and position of printed area, even colour must conform to Post Office requirements.

A final thought, at least for small specialist shots. Actually putting a postage stamp on the reply envelope, rather than using a printed reply-paid format, can double responses. Clearly it costs more, you pay for all the reply envelopes you send out rather than only those that come back, but a new client may be worth more.

Coding, Testing And Measurement

Having touched on the reply vehicle, as this is primarily what provides feedback it seems an appropriate place to pause and consider the monitoring of direct mail activity.

One of the advantages of direct mail is its ability to be tested, and fine-tuned as a result, easily and at low cost.

The reply card can be coded to either the list used, or the mailing material, or both. In other words different versions of the mailing can be used and a check kept on how the response varies. If different batches of reply card are produced with variations they can be sorted and checked on receipt. The code may literally be a code, batches A and B (with A or B printed in the corner); or the address may be varied Department X or Y and so on. In this way not only can immediate response be measured but, longer term, conversion rates can be checked too. It could be that in monitoring two lists, one produces twice as many initial responses but the quality of prospect and conversion rate make it less effective.

In terms of the detail of the mailing if split runs are used a variety of comparisons may be made. This can be well worth checking and you should never underestimate the difference minor changes – which you may even regard as cosmetic – can make.

For example check factors such as these, one against another:

Copy:	long	vs	short
	punchy	vs	conversational
Colour:	one	vs	another
	black/white	vs	one colour
Reply Vehicle:	card	vs	form
	stamp	vs	reply-paid
	send business card	vs	fill in form
Cost (fees):	reference to fees	vs	not
Service	specific service	vs	range of services
Illustrations	include	vs	not
	photographs	vs	line drawings
Offering	further information	vs	straight to meeting
	event as first contact	vs	one to one meeting

In fact any variable element can be tested in this way continuously over time. Because this process inevitably makes for complications at origination and production stages, it is often neglected. The possible improvement of results that can be created as this kind of data base builds up can however make the time and effort involved well worthwhile.

And what sort of results can you expect?

Response rates from direct mail vary enormously. In some fields companies make a good living from response rates of less than 1 per cent, in others 50 per cent may be achieved. In accountancy there is little experience as yet, and less published. It may be useful, and encouraging, therefore to quote Cheryl Gillan, who is in charge of Tax Marketing at Arthur Young, commenting on a particular campaign:

'In order to pull together a group of prospects for certain aspects of our service, we were running a seminar concerned with the relocation of personnel. We decided to use a specifically tailored list of senior Japanese businessmen, in organizations that would obviously have reasonable movement of personnel on an international basis. We sent them a personalized letter detailing the contents of the conference and it resulted in an acceptance rate of between 30 per cent and 40 per cent of the original list mailed. The total list was not large, probably being about 150 in number. I believe that this shows that if you choose your audience very carefully, and are producing an event in which they are most likely to have an interest, that this is where direct mail is particularly useful'.

Costing and Timing

Because there are a variety of elements that make up the total it is essential to work out costs carefully. Prepare a costing sheet, along the lines of the one shown in Figure 1, so that you know in advance what will be involved. Do not forget those costs incurred after the material has been posted, prompt, efficient and effective action when a reply is received also costs money.

If you are a first time direct mail user, then talk to the Post Office, who have a number of attractive start up schemes, including one allowing you to send a first quantity post free.

As well as keeping a close eye and written note of costs, the schedule of timings can also be usefully recorded in calendar style. Copy has to be written, brochures designed and printed, overprinted envelopes need a longer lead time when ordered, and if you are contracting out the collation, insertion and posting this also needs a little time. And so on. If you are working back from a planned arrival date – perhaps you want

Item	£ Cost overall	£ per 000

brochure   – copy
               – design
               – printing		

Letter – copy/layout – printing		
Envelopes		
Reply mechanism – design/print		
Reply-paid (estimate)		

Mailing
 	
  – collating
  – staping
  – folding
  – inserting into envelopes/sealing etc
  – POSTAGE – First Class
                – Second Class
  – rebate sorting (saving £)		

Split-run, additional cost –
            brochure
            letter
            reply mechanism
            envelopes		

Other enclosures –
           –
           –
Follow up costs
eg Brochures/publications
Event   – venue
           – catering
           – documentation		

Misc:		
TOTAL		
Never forget the largest cost may well be *your time.*		

Figure 1 Costing Sheet

this to be exactly a week after the Budget, or 4 weeks before a planned seminar – even the time in the post needs estimating. Always include yourself on the list, maybe sending one to your own office, one to your home, and those of one or two colleagues, so that you can monitor exactly when people receive your promotion. And always circulate material internally well ahead of posting, together with any briefing and a special note to those who will be involved in response action once replies start to arrive. It gives quite the wrong impression if recipients telephone saying they want more information about something they have seen in a mail-shot and the switchboard (or worse still a Partner) can only say 'what mailshot?' Such 'own goals' must be avoided or impact is diluted and possible new business may go by default.

Creativity

Creativity to Order

Creativity is about making things look different. Perhaps in the context of direct mail and accounting, it is about making things which are essentially similar appear different. As such there can be no magic formula either for 'being creative' or, much less, for creating the 'perfect' direct mail promotion. By definition it involves seeking new approaches, rather than slavishly following a format. This section sets out some principles, and floats some ideas. But it is essentially concerned with prompting an approach that will focus the thinking in the right way, allow you to devise approaches that will create interest and give you an edge on competition rather than 'script' things for you. Suggestions are clearly not appropriate for every circumstance and it is certainly not suggested that every factor should be built into every promotion. The trick is in finding a fresh approach and a permutation of approaches that will put over your message in a persuasive manner.

Definition of the Brief

First make some notes, and start by reviewing the whole promotional message rather than one component, the letter say, and get absolutely straight in your mind what the overall message is to be. Particularly ask yourself how what you have to say is new, unique or at least different from the way others may present themselves. To whom *exactly* is it aimed? and is this a sufficiently discreet group? If you try to appeal to too broad a spectrum of recipients at once, you may end up not interesting any of them because the message is not sufficiently specific. Clearly rather different approaches, even tone, will be necessary for existing clients and others.

You must decide whether you are presenting the firm, or particular aspects of it and if it is the latter what aspects you will pick. Is it of topical relevance? Can you describe it in terms of advantages, benefits; if it includes service can you describe exactly what this means? What are you going to say about costs? – value for money – what guarantees, proof, testimonials can you offer. And bearing in mind that the route to action is also important how can you make the asked for action attractive?

Put this down on paper in note form, not aiming for final copy, and try to think objectively how it will appeal. Is it the best possible approach? Would it interest *you*? If not you may need to think of additional 'hooks', elements that will generate the interest you want. By focusing attention. For example:

Combinations	– featuring two things linked together – a budget analysis and action plan.
Team response	– Something to be responded to by more than one person – a meeting designed for the Managing Director and his Finance Director to attend together.
Limited offer	– only a limited number: – can attend – of this publication is available.
Status	– offering people the opportunity to be the first with something, meeting at a prestige venue, meeting local opinion leaders.
A competition	– The prize may be the product, for example in promoting personal financial planning a draw for everyone responding might offer a free consultation, or year's assistance to the winner.
Sponsorship	– link to an event, perhaps a charitable event, 'meet us on such and such a date, and join us at the local theatre club where we are sponsoring the production of ... in the evening'.

Highlight the list source	– if you are using someone else's list you can opt to feature the link – 'as a member of ...', 'as an investor with...'
Second chance	– mail people a second time as a 'reminder' or increasing the appeal.

Through aspects of the overall message for example:

Timing	– an offer that will give benefit
	— 'before the Budget'
	— 'by the end of the year'

Exclusivity	– an offer to a select group
	– 'only for clients'
	– 'only for local businessmen'
	– 'only for farmers in Sussex'

Something free	– before any commitment: a free publication, consultation, or free attendance on a seminar. (These can be linked ie the free publication is only distributed to those who attend the meeting and thus hear more of your proposition.)

Though some accountants admit to doing a good deal more that this to encourage prospective clients, you may want to consider carefully what you would say promotionally about such practice.

Something that must be paid for – a publication, consultation or attendance on a seminar.

Even a nominal charge will give a different quality of response and produce less time wasters with no real intention of pursuing their interest. Or you can charge but offer money back if they are not satisfied – 'if you do not feel two hours spent at our seminar is worthwhile we will refund the fee'. Or deduct it from money spent in future.

Deluxe version – offering something, say a budget analysis, with a better, longer, more detailed version only for those replying to the mailing.

Such factors as these are clearly not mutually exclusive. They can be linked, added to – and no doubt bettered. No one knows yet what degree of gimmick will appeal, be careful of course but remember the recipients probably take a less censorious view than you of such matters. A degree of experiment may well prove worthwhile and, if you are not prepared to be a pioneer, keep a sharp eye on what is done by others. Finally look carefully at *your* particular situation – what is there you can offer simply by taking advantage of circumstances? For example one insurance company sent out a promotion to an explanatory event. With offices in the town centre, they offered coffee and use of their car park on a Saturday – 'spend an hour with us while your wife goes shopping'. A simple, clever idea – they got through a lot of coffee.

Finally keep in mind the things people may obtain from your services. If they will:

- make more money
- save money
- save time, effort or hassle
- be more secure
- sort problems
- exploit opportunities
- motivate their staff
- impress their customers
- persuade others more readily (their bank manager?)

you will need to say so. And if they will do it quicker, easier, more cost-effectively or more anything else say that too. If you believe you provide a worthwhile service, if you believe it is of real value, have the courage of your convictions and say so. If reading your promotion does not clearly show the reader you believe, why ever should they do so?

With all this in mind you can begin to get real copy down on paper. There are two key aspects to this, the words, (the tone, language and approach you use) and the structure into which you fit them to complete the message.

Finding the Words

The point about keeping it simple has already been made. It stands repeating. So use short words, use short sentences, and short paragraphs.

Do not use too much jargon; at worst this will kill a message stone dead, at best it will dilute the message. But as Bernard Shaw said '...the only golden rule is that there are no golden rules'.

This means nothing to excess. Sometimes you *will* need a

longer word, a long sentence and some judiciously chosen jargon.

Two other approaches should pervade the text. First, it should be written from the client's, or potential client's point of view. As such it will say 'you' more than 'I' and 'we'; probably much more. Count them, and especially beware of sentences – and thus points – that start with 'I' or 'we'. It is the quickest way to give the text an introspective feel. Secondly, it must be positive. It should say 'this *is* the case', 'this will be what is done' and will rarely say things like 'I think …', 'probably' or 'may be'.

Experienced direct mailers talk about 'magic' words, or at least words that inject a tone that should always be present. These include – free, guarantee, new, announcing, you, now, today, win, easy, save, at once – you must not overuse them or the message will become blatantly 'over the top', but do not neglect them either.

You must search constantly for ways of making your copy perform better. Again the following is designed not only to float some examples but to show the approach you need to cultivate.

The guidelines that follow are reviewed in terms of 'do's' and 'don'ts', with no apology for the occasional repetition this produces.

Don'ts
You should not:
—*be too clever* It is the argument that should win the reader round, not the flowery phrases, elegant quotations or clever approach.
—*be too complicated* The point about simplicity has been made. It applies equally to the overall argument.
—*be pompous* This means too much about you, your firm and your services (instead of what it means to them). It means writing in a way that is too far removed from the way you would speak. It means too slavishly following the exact grammar at the expense of an easy flowing style).
—*overclaim* While you should certainly have the courage of your convictions, too many superlatives can become self defeating. One claim that seems doubtful and the whole argument suffers.
—*offer opinions* Or at least not too many compared with the statement of facts, ideally substantiated facts.
—*lead into points with negatives:* For example, do not say 'If this

is not the case we will ...', rather 'You will find ... or ...'

—*assume your reader lacks knowledge:* Rather than saying for example, 'You probably do not know that ...' Better, 'many people have not yet heard...'

—*overdo humour* Never use humour in fact unless you are very sure of it. An inward groan as they read does rather destroy the nodding agreement you are trying to build. A quotation or quip, particularly if it is relevant, is safer and even if the humour is not appreciated, the appropriateness may be noted.

—*use up benefits early* A direct mail letter must not run out of steam, it must end on a high note and still be talking in terms of benefits even towards and at the end.

Now some Do's

— *concentrate on facts* This relates to the 'don't' about opinions, the case you put over must be credible and factual. A clear cut, 'these are all the facts you need to know' approach tends to pay dividends in professional services.

—*use captions* While pictures, illustrations or photographs and charts can often be regarded as speaking for themselves, they will have more impact if used with a caption. (This can be a good way of achieving acceptable repetition, mention in the text and in the caption.)

—*use repetition* Key points can appear more than once, in the leaflet and the letter, even more than once in the letter itself. This applies, of course, especially to benefits.

—*keep changing the language* Get yourself a Thesaurus. You need to find numbers of·ways of saying the same thing in brochures and letters and so on.

—*say what is new* Assuming you have something new, novel – even unique – to say, make sure the reader knows it. Real differentiation can often be lost, in the quantity of words make sure the key points stand out.

—*address the recipient* You must do so accurately and precisely. You must know exactly who you are writing to, what their needs, likes, dislikes are and be ever-conscious of tailoring the message. Too far towards being all things to all people will dilute the effectiveness to any one recipient.

—*keep them reading* Consider breaking sentences at the end of a page so that they have to turn over to complete the sentence. (Yes, it does not look quite so nice, but it works.) Always make it clear that other pages do follow, putting 'continued...' or similar at the foot of the page.

—*link paragraphs* Again to keep them reading. Use 'horse and cart' points to carry the argument along. For example one paragraph starts 'One example of this is...', the next starts 'Now let's look at how that works...'

—*be descriptive* Really descriptive. In words, a system may be better described as 'smooth as silk' than 'very straightforward to operate'. Remember, *you* know how good what you are describing is, they do not. You need to tell them and must not assume they will catch your enthusiasm from a brief phrase.

—*involve people* First your people. Do not say '...the head of our Audit Division', say 'John Smith, the head of our Audit Division'. And other people. Do not say '...it is a proven service...', say ...'more than 300 clients have found it satisfactory...'

—*add credibility* For example if you quote users, quote names (with their permission) – if you quote figures quote them specifically – mention people by name. Being specific adds to credibility, do not say 'this is described in our booklet on venture capital...', rather '...this is described on page 16 of our booklet on venture capital...'

—*use repetition* Key points can appear more than once, in the leaflet and the letter, even more than once in the letter itself. This applies, of course, especially to benefits repeated for emphasis, (you will notice this paragraph is repeated, either to show the technique works or perhaps to demonstrate that half hearted attempts at humour are not altogether recommended).

A final comment in this section concerns editing. Edit, edit, edit (more repetition). It is usually easier to start with more copy than you need and edit it back to length, improving it as you go, rather than adding to a short draft. In addition it may need going over more than once and time spent in 'fine-tuning' is often worth while. This is different from trying to incorporate the views of everyone else among the partners or on the marketing committee; which leads conveniently to organization.

Creativity and Organization

Partnerships are essentially democratic. Promotional activity is essentially creative. The two sit uneasily together. Everyone knows the story of the committee that set out to design a horse and ended up with a camel. On subjective matters, this effect is most pronounced. Take a simple example, the practice letterhead. Everyone may have different ideas of what is right, and on one level it is a matter of opinion. Yet what matters, all that matters, is how clients and prospective clients will see it. Will it stike them as up to date, effective, even novel, or will it end up as a compromize, various elements diluted so that every possible objection and view is accommodated *internally* but impact is lost externally?

There is no easy answer. But it does stand some thought. Such matters must be centred on one, or certainly fewer, people if decisions are going to be made that promote persuasiveness and are made promptly.

It cannot, for whatever reason, all be done internally then, support must be sought elsewhere.

Outside Assistance

Design, preparation and particularly writing any part of the direct mail package is crucial, well worth some time and money and possibly some professional assistance. One firm whom my own company recently assisted with the rewriting and design of their corporate brochure felt it worth adding half as much again to a print bill of between £3–4000. This does not mean small inputs from outside, at less cost, are impossible, they are not, and they can help.

The total process is perhaps more complex than might seem the case at first sight. One company, where they know a thing or two about work in this kind of area, use a chart to illustrate the process of those with whom they work. It shows the sequence of events involved in producing a brochure (intended in fact for recruitment purposes, but the process is similar for any other item). The complexity and importance of detail is immediately apparent. Only by handling such a project systematically will the end result stand a chance of achieving its objectives.

Every item is different but a systematic approach is necessary to planning a job-specific schedule (see the flow chart in Figure 1, Chapter 4).

You may well do all this yourself, liaising direct with a printer. On the other hand you may need professional assistance. Assistance may be needed with copy (the words used in the material), with design and graphics (how the material will look); artwork must be prepared for a printer to work from; a printer and printing process must be selected and proofs checked; colours matched etc.

In either case the process of choosing the right assistance is crucial. In selecting a printer, describe the job you want done, look at work he has done before, ask how long it will take. As much of the print business works on a jobbing basis it may be useful to know how much of the work he will do himself. With an agency or freelancer on the 'creative' side, who will be concerned with design, graphics, copy etc, you are really seeking a partner in the implementation of a part of your marketing strategy. Again look at what they have done in the past and for whom. Ask how well it worked, has that client come back to them for more, can you check personally with a satisfied client? Making the right choice is an important decision, and it may well be worth seeing a number of people. Final judgement may well be influenced by those elements of the job with which you need most help; for example the fact that it is easier to find someone who will make a brochure look nice than someone who will ensure its overall message, the words and way it is presented meet your objectives, and that it will therefore do a really persuasive job on those who see it. With direct mail copy this is perhaps the key, (not that other things are unimportant!) and help with this may be useful. Only you can start the process, think through what needs to be said and perhaps do the first draft, so do not overestimate how much of the time of the job you can shed through delegating to an outside agency.

In other areas you may need list brokers (who can provide the names) and mailing houses (who physically get the shot into the post) – sometimes companies do both. There seems little point in having your staff stuffing envelopes, when time is no doubt already at a premium.

Conclusion

Direct mail is a recent addition to the promotional techniques available to accountants in practice. Although it is a late entrant to your promotional mix, it may well prove an important one. Certainly experience of other professional services, some not a million miles removed from accountancy, suggests this is likely. It is used elsewhere. It works. And it does not seem to antagonize recipients in the process. It lends itself to the kind of limited, cost-effective, and continuous promotional campaigns accountants see as increasingly necessary. This does not preclude wider scale use by the larger firms, it is potentially useful at every level.

It therefore presents an opportunity to better develop the practice. On the other side an inevitable consequence is that an increased amount of promotion will be visible out in the market perhaps contributing to a further increase in the prevailing competitiveness which faces the accountancy world. As a result while the client is presented with more information, more choice; the accountant has more demanding clients, faces more new client situations in competition and sees established client relationships continuing to be more vulnerable than in the past. The degree of threat depends in part on the effectiveness with which existing client relationships are managed (see Chapter 7). By proper management you can make suggestions to existing clients before they arrive on his desk as direct mail from elsewhere and make him think 'why didn't my accountant suggest that'.

Finally, while direct mail adds to the complexity of the promotional mix, and exhibits special factors to be taken into account in its use – as I hope this chapter has shown – it is in fact simply another promotional mechanism. For all the controversy that has, in some quarters, forerun its inclusion among permitted techniques, for all the emotive reactions it tends to generate, it is, in intention, no different to other kinds of advertising.

It seeks to inform, and to do so persuasively. While it must of course do so in a way that is acceptable to its recipients, its ultimate objective is to produce more business. To do this it must be genuinely persuasive, creating anything else less is a waste of time and money. Ensuring it is persuasive needs an open mind, a creative approach, and attention to detail. As has been described small changes, additions, nuance can make a real difference to results. One thing is described for certain, even for those who perhaps at this stage disapprove of direct mail – it cannot be ignored. It will be used and, provided it proves successful (and who would confidently predict that it will not), it will join the existing promotional techniques as a further element in the armoury that can be deployed to win more business and grow the practice.

Direct mail certainly presents the accountant with the opportunity, and, as I said in the Preface 'the trouble with opportunities is that they so often come disguised as hard work'. Those that take the time and trouble to understand it and use it will give themselves a slight, but significant, edge over those who do not.

Chapter 6

Personal Selling

'We are all salesmen
everyday of our lives'
Charles M Schwab

As has been mentioned, none of the promotional techniques reviewed will actually do the complete job of securing new business. They produce enquiries. Only the personal element, persuasive personal selling, can successfully convert the enquiries into clients.

Yet how many in the profession went into it in order to sell things? Perhaps it is a more pointed question to ask how many went into it in order to avoid the necessity to sell things? So if the word 'marketing' is replaced euphemistically by 'practice developments', how much more suspect in the professional world of accountancy is the word 'selling'? It may be more acceptable to speak in terms of customer contact skills and processes, but there is no way of disguising the intention. That is to sell.

Both the 'professional' and the 'service' elements of accountancy make the detailed adoption of those marketing techniques that are appropriate a matter of some care. (So do any rules governing the ethical conduct of the business obtaining process.) This is important and especially so in the area of selling.

Everything now dealt with can be used in contact with:

- existing clients (those already worked for and their colleagues in the same company);
- enquirers (those who take the initiative and make the first contact requesting information, advice or discussion); and, as appropriate with
- intermediaries (those who can recommend accountancy services to others, eg banks; this is a category identified in the ethical guidelines).

The word 'prospect' is used to indicate people who might have need of a firm's services but are not yet clients. It does *not* imply people to whom a cold approach has been made, indeed that is presently an unethical practice.

Business does have to be obtained. If no action at all is taken, the chances are the world will not beat a path to any organization's door, and if it is to grow and prosper it must take action to ensure that the revenue it gains exceeds its cost. The business of accountancy services is no different from any other in this respect.

Services can seldom be tried out, inspected, or tested in advance. Prospective buyers are, therefore, forced to rely on surrogates to assess what they are likely to get, for example, brochures, other clients, even premises.

People use appearances to make judgements about realities. Thus, the less tangible the product, the more powerfully and persistently the judgement about it is shaped by its packaging – how it is presented, who presents it, and, not least, who sells it.

If the business is booked, whether with a new client or with the extension of work for an existing client, it is likely that some sort of sales activity has in fact taken place.

While the fact that selling takes place and the need for it is not in doubt, *how* the sales process is conducted may be. Professional people must be able to conduct the sales process professionally, because they owe it to their clients to communicate their recommendations as persuasively as possible.

One of the key organizational problems to be solved in a service firm, where the 'production' and 'sales' resources tend to be the same people, is how the appropriate amount of each resource can be put behind each function. Time must be made available so that the right people can sell at the right time.

Any consideration of sales technique makes best sense if we start by considering the buyer's point of view. Why do people buy accountancy services? They do so to satisfy needs, both objective and subjective. Key needs include:

- problems that need to be solved;
- opportunities that need to be exploited;
- difficult judgement decisions that have to be taken;
- workloads that have to be handled;
- other people who have to be convinced.

Such needs can exist singly or together, and are satisfied by the major *benefits* (results) that are produced for clients.

These benefits are proved by the features of the firm; the facts about its staff, history and past client successes.

The concept of Need — Benefit — Feature is fundamental to all sales processes.

Furthermore, the client must be convinced not only that he is being offered the general benefits of professional advice, but also a much more precise service.

He is looking for assurance; first that the benefits can be addressed to the *specific* problems/opportunities that he is facing in his business. Secondly, that the accountants to whom he is talking are themselves capable of understanding his problems/opportunities and of rendering the appropriate service.

Thus he will be best persuaded by professionals who can sell, rather than by professional salesmen. In accountancy the 'people' are the 'product'.

The Process of the Sale

Selling is a process of thrusting stimuli into the client in order to cause responses which lead ultimately to a buying decision. This process normally goes through a series of stages:

Attention

People tend to be most attentive when talking about themselves, their situation or their problems, or listening to topics which directly relate to their problems.

Interest

Interest is generated when having identified, understood and accepted his own needs, the buyer begins to see that what seller is telling him relates to those needs.

Desire

The buyer now wants the 'product', both objectively and subjectively, since he is able to see that his needs can be satisfied.

Action

In order to satisfy those needs he must now take buying action, which most people find difficult without some help from the seller.

Selling is a series of social skills aimed at modifying buying behaviour. These skills come naturally to very few people; most people have to learn and practise them to become proficient.

The range and type of skill that can usefully be used will vary from one client situation to another.

The successful accountant will therefore first identify the situation that he is in, in order to select the appropriate skills and techniques to be used, and most important of all will prepare in advance how he will sell, as well as what he is going to sell.

Because 'the people are the product', he cannot escape from the responsibility of being able to sell. It is an intrinsic part of being successful.

The Buying Process

Buying is simply an action that satisfies a need; that is a means to achieve objectives, a goal, ambition or end result. Conversely, people will not buy if they do not have a need, are not aware that they do, or recognize it but not strongly enough to take action.

There are many kinds and combinations of need. These include single/multiple; strong/weak; superior/subordinate; past/present/future; frequent/occasional; objective/subjective; individual/group; personal/job related and public/private needs. This must be recognized, as must the fact that different people will take the same action, but for different reasons, for example in booking a package holiday to Majorca. Conversely, different people will take different actions, but for the same reasons, as with different ways to impress the neighbours.

How do people buy? Some needs are satisfied by instinctive reactions, some by habit, others by conscious thought. However, decisions to act or not to act on the requests of other people are taken by the following process:

1 *I am important and want to be respected*
↓
2 *Consider my needs*
↓
3 *Will your ideas help me?*
↓
4 *What are the facts?*
↓
5 *What are the snags?*
↓
6 *What shall I do?*
↓
7 *I approve/disapprove*

Each step in the process must be cleared before the buying mind will willingly move on to the next one. Some decisions can be taken at once, while others require a pause between each stage.

In buying professional services, decisions follow the same seven-step process, but execution of the process can be much more complex due to the nature of the client's business; the size of the organization; the people and functions involved; their needs, and the degree of influence they have on buying decisions.

Selling is a process of need satisfaction and research shows two facts that are extremely valuable to sellers, first that interviews are *much more successful* when the client states his needs. Secondly, as a result, they are *less successful* when his needs are only *implied*.

Nothing is successfully sold unless a client willingly buys. This is encouraged by offering satisfied needs as reasons for buying, ie, perfect holes, not precision drills; reduced administrative costs, not computer programs. To follow the buying mind's seven-step process, and to achieve all this requires planning what to do in advance.

Sales Planning

Planning of overall sales activity has been referred to earlier as part of the complete marketing plan. Here the process of planning an individual approach, whether to sell on to an existing client or an initial approach to a new contact, is examined. This kind of planning is a vital prerequisite of a succesful sales approach.

Why? The face-to-face interview is a key element of the whole approach; failure here normally means total failure, the initiative cannot be taken further. Additionally, while there are many similarities between different prospects and clients, each of them considers himself unique, and rightly expects a tailored approach. Selling time is precious for both parties. Both have commercial objectives, but normally the accountant's need to sell is greater than the client's need to buy. For these reasons all calls need to be planned, whether such calls are on existing clients, on prospects, on minor opportunities, or on major opportunities.

There are seven steps in call planning on existing clients:

(1) Objectives;
(2) Research;
(3) Opening;
(4) Presentation;
(5) Objections;
(6) Close;
(7) Equipment.

See Sales checklist number 1.

The major problem in calling on prospects is lack of information, and often there is no previous relationship to which reference can be made, so the emphasis is, therefore, on pre-call research and opening.

This only formalizes the 'thinking first, acting second' principle to ensure that subsequent discussions with the 'prospect' (be he existing client or enquirer) proceed purposefully. (See Sales checklist number 2.)

Where a major project is possible, there are additional considerations to be borne in mind. Major sales are time consuming, complex, risky, and expensive. The rewards for success and the penalties of failure can be enormous (eg, computer installations). Such purchases often mean big changes to a prospect's business, involving both operational and financial analyses, and the willing agreement of many people in different functions.

Success in these situations, therefore, requires involvement in the prospect's business, contact with all who affect the final decision, identification of their specific needs, and satisfaction of their operation and financial requirements. Again planning, or the lack of it, makes all the difference. While no two major sales situations are the same, the similarities are numerous enough to produce an eight-stage approach:

(1) Pre-call analysis;
(2) Survey of client situation;
(3) Identification of client needs;
(4) Development of solution;
(5) Operational and financial justification;
(6) Verbal agreement;
(7) Written confirmation;
(8) Commitment.

Sales checklist number 1: Call planning – existing clients

	Yes	No
(1) Are my *objectives:*		
• stated as client needs?		
• commercially worthwhile?		
• consistent with our policy?		
• achievable within our resources?		
• measurable?		
• timed?		
(2) Have I done enough *research* on:		
• the person to be seen?		
• the client's situation?		
• recommenders?		
• influencers?		
• supporters?		
• their needs?		
• competition?		
(3) Will my *opening*:		
• put him at ease?		
• get him interested and talking?		
• explore his needs?		
• establish his priorities?		
(4) Will my *presentation*:		
• offer him desirable results from his point of view?		
• prove my case to his satisfaction?		
• explain complex points simply?		
• show how his needs can be met?		
(5) If he raises *objections*:		
• have I considered what they might be?		
• have I got answers which will satisfy him?		
• are they related to his needs?		
(6) Will my *close*:		
• get a commitment?		
• match my objectives?		
• make it easy for him to agree?		
• leave him feeling better than before the call?		
(7) In terms of *equipment*:		
• have I identified what I will need?		
• have I identified what he may need?		
• have I got it with me?		
• have I decided how to use it?		

Each stage contains a number of key points that have to be covered (see Sales checklist number 3).

Finally, in planning, there is the need for the longer term view, a 'client strategy' for those major clients, which in most firms produce a significant proportion of total fees and, hopefully, profit. Such clients, because of their complexity and power, are different in nature as well as size. They are not like all other clients, only bigger. This can rapidly be demonstrated by considering the effect of losing one. It is, therefore, vital that the relationship with them proceeds purposefully over a long period and this normally means planning at least a year ahead. Thus, the elements to be considered in developing a Major Client Strategy of this sort include:

(1) Contacts in the client;
(2) Contacts in the practice;
(3) Assignment analysis last year, including trends;
(4) Competitive activity, and relative strengths and weaknesses, in terms of service, fees and terms, and 'presentation';
(5) Next year's objectives;
(6) Overall strategy statement;
(7) Detailed action plans –
   • contacts to be made
   • objectives of calls
   • support required
   • timing and deadlines.

Current trends seem to indicate that major clients and the way they are managed will, in future, form an increasingly important part of a firm's work. To manage them well, the accountant will need a broad appreciation of business; planning skills and systems; coordinating ability; financial techniques, and negotiating skills. (See Chapter 7.)

Observation shows that call planning tends to be a weak area. Strengths can be maximized in face-to-face situations by thorough planning, so that the possibility of client rejection caused by unforeseen errors is reduced to a minimum.

Using the seven-step buying process discussed earlier, the thorough planning of a sales approach can be turned into a real and effective approach.

Sales checklist number 2: Call planning – prospects

	Yes	No
(1) *Objectives:* – See Sales checklist number 1.		

(2) Have I done enough *research* on:

	Yes	No
● background information on this prospect?	_____	_____
–published sources?	_____	_____
–prospect sources?	_____	_____
–other sources?	_____	_____
● backgound information on his industry?	_____	_____
–published sources?	_____	_____
–prospect sources?	_____	_____
–other sources?	_____	_____
● backgound information on his competition?	_____	_____
–published sources?	_____	_____
–prospect sources?	_____	_____
–other sources?	_____	_____
● possible needs?	_____	_____
● major needs?	_____	_____
● future plans?	_____	_____
● whether there is an obvious need for my services?	_____	_____
● whether it has sales potential?	_____	_____

See Sales checklist number 1.

(3) Will my *opening:*

	Yes	No
● fill gaps in essential knowledge?	_____	_____
–buying process?	_____	_____
–decision makers?	_____	_____
–industry situation?	_____	_____
–company situation?	_____	_____
–organization?	_____	_____
–needs?	_____	_____
–competition?	_____	_____
–his?	_____	_____
–ours?	_____	_____
● impress him about me?	_____	_____
● impress him about the company?	_____	_____

See Sales checklist number 1.

(4) *Presentation* –See Sales checklist number 1.
(5) *Objections* –See Sales checklist number 1.
(6) *Close* –See Sales checklist number 1.
(7) *Equipment* –See Sales checklist number 1.

The Accountant's Guide to Practice Promotion

Sales checklist number 3: Planning a major sale

A 'no' answer to any of the questions should be resolved before proceeding.

	Yes	No
(1) *Pre-call analysis*		
(1.1) Do I know enought about this prospect and his industry?	_____	_____
(1.2) Is anything extra needed?	_____	_____
(1.3) Do I have some idea of his possible problems and needs?	_____	_____
(2) *Survey of client situation*		
(2.1) Have I identified the decision maker?	_____	_____
(2.2) Do I know his possible problems and needs?	_____	_____
(2.3) Is there agreement in principle to proceed?	_____	_____
(2.4) Have they agreed to let us survey their operation?	_____	_____
(3) *Identification of client needs*		
(3.1) Have I identified all the individuals/ departments who will be affected by a purchase/ non-purchase decision?	_____	_____
(3.2) Do I know their needs?	_____	_____
(3.3) Do they recognize the importance of their needs?	_____	_____
(3.4) Have I got all the facts to justify my solution both operationally and financially?	_____	_____
(3.5) Have I involved all those who will be affected?	_____	_____
(4) *Development of solution*		
Does my solution meet the various needs?	_____	_____
(4.2) Will it meet the priority needs?	_____	_____
(4.3) Will it cause any major problems for the clients?	_____	_____
(4.4) Will it cause any major problems for us?	_____	_____
(4.5) Is it likely to be accepted?	_____	_____
(5) *Operational and financial justification*		
(5.1) Do I know where my solution will have greatest effect?	_____	_____
• buying/accounts?	_____	_____
• production?	_____	_____
• marketing and sales?	_____	_____
• R and D?	_____	_____
• personnel?	_____	_____
(5.2) Can I quantify the effects?	_____	_____
(5.3) Do they offer significant improvements?	_____	_____
(5.4) Have I calculated and produced the relevant figures?	_____	_____

	Yes	No
(6) *Verbal agreement*		
(6.1) Does everyone accept the operational and financial arguments?	_____	_____
(6.2) Any problems?	_____	_____
(6.3) Problems resolved?	_____	_____
(7) *Written confirmation*		
(7.1) Do I know who should receive/read my formal confirmation?	_____	_____
(7.2) Do I know which method of confirmation will be most effective?	_____	_____
(7.3) Does it contain everything needed by the readers to gain their acceptance?	_____	_____
(8) *Commitment*		
(8.1) Should I present the written confirmation?	_____	_____
(8.2) Having presented, did I get acceptance?	_____	_____
(8.3) Did I answer all questionns/objections?	_____	_____
(8.4) Has the commitment been implemented?	_____	_____

Analysing Client Needs

Client attitudes vary at the beginning of interviews. They can be friendly, hostile, indifferent, interested, helpful or defensive, and the opening of an interview is therefore a crucial time for both parties.

Remember the first two steps in the buying process:

1 *I am important and want to be respected*

2 *Consider my needs*

These two steps make the accountant's objectives at the beginning of an interview very clear:
- to make the client feel important in the accountant's eyes; and
- to agree to the client's stated needs.

Successful selling is particularly dependent on this stage in the buying process being well handled. Exploring, identifying and agreeing to the client's needs correctly makes him want to hear the proposition. Subsequently, making it attractive reduces the possibility of objections and thus obtains more voluntary commitments.

Remember people act to relieve a felt need. Where the need is low, the solution has a low impact, where the need is high, the solution has a high impact, either positively or negatively depending on the way it is offered. Sometimes, clients will volunteer their needs and priorities. More often, needs have to be explored and identified before they can be agreed and priorities set.

Exploration can be done by either questions or statements or by a combination of both questions and statements. Questions are initially safer and more productive, but they have to be carefully and correctly used. The precise method of questioning technique most likely to bring results utilizes four basic types of question:

- *Background questions*
  For example, 'what's your unit cost per item?'
- *Problem questions*
  For example, 'are unit costs a problem?'
- *Implications questions*
  For example, 'what effect are high unit costs having on the rest of the business?'

- *Need questions*
  For example, 'what would you like to happen as far as unit costs are concerned?'

Open or closed questions can be equally successful, but open questions (that cannot be answered with 'yes' or 'no') encourage the client to talk and produce more information.

The type and combination of questions used is very important. Experience shows that asking fewer background questions but focusing them better, asking more problem questions, amplifying problems by asking implications questions and converting problems and implications into need questions works best and forms a logical sequence.

Whereas asking a relatively large number of background questions, fewer problem, implications or need questions, and introducing solutions after the stage of asking background questions works less well.

The reason for this difference in success rate is very simple. The first follows the client's buying sequence, the latter makes accountants talk about themselves, their companies, and their services which distances the approach from the client.

Each type of question has an equivalent approach based on a statement.

The same sequence can be used as with questions, that is: Background—Problems—Implications—Needs, and statements can be most confidently used when the accountant already has a thorough understanding of the client's situation. Thus, they are more often used after questioning or during subsequent calls.

Clients with strongly felt needs will often buy with very little encouragement. Many clients, however, are satisfied with existing solutions. They will maintain the status quo unless something causes them to become dissatisfied. Accountants faced with this situation must, in fact, create some dissatisfaction before the client will consider a change. This must be done without criticising the client's previous decisions, which may well make him defensive. This can most readily be done by showing that due to factors outside his control, the situation is unsatisfactory. Many outside factors can be used in this way: other people's actions and attitudes; the behaviour of materials, products or systems; market forces and local, national or world events; natural phenomena like the weather and many others.

Clients will normally have a mix of needs and rarely will they be equally important. The next stage, as a client's needs are established, is to identify and agree their priority. Questions that will establish this must, therefore, be included in the early stages of conversation.

This early stage is vital, as the old saying has it, 'you get only one chance to make a good first impression'. Not only are clients making judgements on competence and approach at this stage, but the success of all that follows is dependent on the information base being established. What precisely is next will be based on this information, and is the first step towards an approach that will differentiate us from our competitors and secure the business in competitive situations.

Offering Solutions

Once needs are identified and priorities established, the next step is to show how satisfaction will come from the specific services or recommendations that are offered. Again the action springs from the appropriate stage of the buying process.

The client's mental demands are:

3   *Will your ideas help me?*

4   *What are the snags?*

This means that the accountant has four objectives: to make his ideas understandable, attractive and convincing, and to get feedback that the first three have been successfully achieved.

Each of these elements can be considered in turn and then have to be deployed together in a cohesive and effective conversation:

Making ideas understandable
Three main factors effect this, they are:

Structure and sequence
Presentations should always be structured around the client's needs.

eg 'So in choosing a system, your first concern is compatibility, your second is simplicity, and your third is productivity. Let's look at the compatibility aspect first, and then deal with the others...'

It is also important to conclude one aspect before moving to the next, and to take matters in a logical order.

Visual Aids

People understand and remember more when information is presented in visual form. Charts, diagrams, slides, pictures and brochures can all strengthen the clarity of the presentation. In using them follow the basic rules, keep them hidden until they are needed, keep quiet while they are being examined (people cannot concentrate on two things at once) and remove after use to avoid any distraction.

Jargon

Every company and industry has its own language or jargon and accountancy is no exception. Some jargon can be useful, if pitched at the right level, but overall the presentation must use the client's language. This means utilizing words and terms which it is certain the client understands and avoiding words or terms which can be misinterpreted in any way, eg 'our service is cheap'.

Making Ideas Attractive

People buy things for what they will do (benefits, that is 'desirable results from the listener's point of view') not for what they *are* (features).

Professional services can do many different things for clients but not all clients want the same things done. Thus, only those benefits which meet the listener's needs should be used and it is the process of selecting and matching items from the total list of benefits to an individual customer's specific requirements that makes a particular idea, or solution, appear attractive.

There are normally three types of benefit which can be used; benefits to the listener is his job, as a person, or benefits to others in which he is interested, and the choice will depend on the listener's needs and priorities.

Making Ideas Convincing

Benefits are claims for the service. Such claims may have to be substantiated, as sales claims are always viewed with some scepticism. This can be done by describing the features which produce them, or by reference to third parties.

Third party references must be used only to support the case, not as arguments in themselves. If a specific third party is named, it should be one respected by the listener, and should face similar conditions to the client. A third party should not just be mentioned, but linked to a description of the particular benefits and need satisfactions that the third party obtained.

Example 3 shows an example of the correct linked use of benefits and features.

EXAMPLE 3   USING BENEFITS AND FEATURES

(a) *Simple statement*   B→F
   For example, 'you will get more assignments if you use Benefits that match the clients's Needs'.

(b) *Comparison statement*   B→F→WA*→NE*
   For example, 'you will get more assignments if you use Benefits that match the client's Needs. Vague or unrelated Benefits have a low impact.

(c) *Sandwich statement*   B→F→WA→NE→F→B
   For example, 'you will get more assignments if you use Benefits that match the client's Needs. Vague or unrelated Benefits have a low impact; but by carefully selecting Benefits that have a strong appeal you will get more business and get it sooner.'

*WA – Wrong Action
*NE – Negative Effect

Obtaining Feedback

To ensure that progress is being made towards the ultimate objective, accurate feedback is necessary all the time. It is then possible to be flexible and readjust as the conversation proceeds. By observation, by waiting and listening to the client's reply, and by asking for a comment, feedback can be assured, and monitoring questions, like the following can constantly be answered:

Am I discussing your Needs?
Is this a problem?
Is my proposition attractive, clear and convincing?
Have I overlooked anything?

This ensures that the clients's needs are being satisfied, keeps the client involved in the discussion, and prevents problems developing later on.

Presenting one's case is simple and successful if one follows these basic rules:

● Take one point at a time.
● Tell the client what it means to him in terms of results.

- Show him what it is or means.
- Provide proof where necessary.
- Check progress by obtaining constant feedback.

Even so there can still be certain problems.

Dealing With Resistance

Instinctively considering possible disadvantages in contemplating an action is a natural human reaction, in selling such considerations pose resistance, though the tendency for this to occur can be reduced. Resistance is more frequent and stronger when needs are insufficiently explored, solutions are offered too soon, or benefits and features are presented too generally.

The majority of objections are not inherent in clients therefore, but are created by the person selling.

Resistance has both an emotional and rational content. Emotionally, the client becomes defensive or aggressive, rationally, he needs a logical answer; these two elements have to be tackled separately and sequentially if resistance is to be overcome.

How? First by keeping your emotions under control, by listening, pausing and thinking, acknowledging his comment – a sort of 'sparring' technique designed to lower the temperature.

Next, rational answers must be provided. It helps to turn the objection into a question, to establish the client's need behind his resistance. Why is he asking this? Is it an excuse? Delaying tactics? Perhaps he does have a point?

Although, 'what are the snags?' is an instinctive part of the buying process, by the time the client reaches this stage he may be sufficiently attracted by the proposal to pass on without raising objections. It pays to concentrate on resistance prevention rather than resistance cure. Agreement on stated needs and careful selection and presentation of need-related benefits reduces both the frequency and strength of resistance.

Obtaining Commitment

Knowing that the objective of all selling is to obtain client commitments often obscures the need to remember how clients arrive at the point of commitment. Clients only willingly take buying decisions after they have recognized and felt needs, and are convinced that their needs will be satisfied by implementing the proposal. Thus, the best chance of success lies in doing a good job before the client reaches the stage of asking himself 'what shall I do?'

Attempts to get commitment (closing) without first having created desire for the proposal will normally be seen by the client as pressure tactics. The bigger the decision, the greater the pressure, and the stronger the client's resistance.

Closing does not cause orders, it merely converts a high desire into orders and a low desire into refusals. Even when a desire is high, however, the client may not *volunteer* a positive commitment. Similarly, the client may want to make a commitment, but there are several variations of it, and the accountant wants one particular kind. It is in these situations that closing skills are valuable; such skills concentrate the buyer's mind on the advantages to be gained from the buying decision itself.

There are certain behaviours, questions and comments indicating a general willingness to buy that can provide 'buying signals'. Tone of voice, posture, hestitation, nodding, questions on details showing acceptance in principle, or comments expressing positive interest are all examples. These can be converted into closes, being careful not to oversell when the client wants to make a commitment.

Although this is the crunch point and can sometimes be avoided because of the unpleasant possibility of getting a 'no', the commitment must actually be asked for; the only question is exactly how it is put. Example 4 shows a variety of ways and examples.

EXAMPLE 4   METHODS OF OBTAINING CLIENT COMMITMENT

Direct request
For example, 'shall we go ahead then and start getting these improvements in service levels?'

This should be used where the client likes to make his own decisions.

Command
For example, 'install this new system in each regional office. It will give you the information you want much more quickly and help you to make more effective use of your transport.'

This can be used where the client:

- has difficulty in making a decision; or
- has considerable respect for the accountant.

Immediate gain

For example, 'you mentioned that this year the company really needs to improve productivity. If you can give me the go-ahead now, I can make sure that you see specific results in three months' time.'

This could be used where, by acting fast, the client can get an important benefit, whereas delay might cause him severe problems.

Alternatives

For example, 'both these approaches meet your criteria. Which one do you prefer to implement?'

This could be used where the accountant is happy to get a commitment on any one of the possible alternatives.

'Best solution'

For example, 'you want a system that can cope with occasional off-peak demands, that is easy to operate by semi-skilled staff and is presented in a form that will encourage line managers to use it. The best fit with all these requirements is our system 'X'. When's the best time to install it?'

This should be used when the client has a mix of Needs, some of which can be better met by the competition, but which when taken as a whole are best met by your solution.

Question or objection

'If we can make that revision, can you get the Finance Director to place the order?'

This should be used where the accountant knows he can answer the client's objection to his satisfaction.

Assumption

'Fine. I've now got all the information I need to meet your requirements. As soon as I get back to the office I'll prepare the necessary paper work and you'll be able to start by the end of next week.'

Concession

Trade only a small concession to get agreement now or agree to proceed only on stage one.

So far so good. The answer at this point may well be 'yes'.

No matter how well a presentation is given and questions handled in selling professional services, the prospect will invariably have some objections to making a decision. Sometimes these objections are stated, but often they are reserved and come in the form – 'I'll think about it'.

When this happens, simple closes may only irritate the prospect and the way forward may be unclear. Yet it is a key stage to get over, and this can be done by listing the objections:

'I agree you should think about it. However, it's probably also your experience that when someone says they want to think about it it's because they are still uncertain about some points. In order to help our thinking on these, let's note them down.' Then make a list with room for more objections than he has, do not write any down until each is understood, and do not answer any—yet. Flush them all out and be sure there are not more to come. This enables an additional closing technique to be used. 'If I'm able to answer each of these points to your complete satisfaction, can we agree we're in business? This is the conditional close. Each point listed is answered in turn, crossed off the list, and the prospect's agreement with each checked, then the close is not repeated, but assumption used to conclude matters: 'Fine, we're in business'.

Having made a commitment, a client may need reassurance that he has done the right thing.

Therefore, always thank him, confirm that he has made a wise decision, touch once more on what will come from it, conclude and leave promptly.

When the client has been satisfied on the first points in the buying process, a close, emphasizing the need satisfaction that a commitment will bring, will naturally convert desire into action.

Good selling can often make formal closing unnecessary: 'make him thirsty and you won't have to force him to drink'.

The sales process described so far will almost always pause, a stage at which written proposals have to be submitted.

Putting it in Writing

The proposal is a tool to help close the sale successfully. By itself, the proposal will not get the order; proposals do not sell, people do, but the proposal can and must help.

A proposal is more complex than a letter. It has to command attention, be understood and is designed to be acted upon. It must put across clearly the technical information necessary – a process that must be done to match the customer's point of view. Too many proposals are written on 'automatic pilot'. Before pen is put to paper it is necessary to think clearly about the intentions for a specific proposal. For whom is the proposal and its message intended? (This is not always only the person to whom it is addressed.) What are their needs? How does your position satisfy those needs – what benefits does it give?

What do you want the prospect to do when he receives the proposal? There must be clear objectives for every proposal, as follows:

- It must be commercially worth while.
- It should be stated in terms of client needs.
- It should be realistic and achievable.
- It must be specific, clear and appropriately timed.
- It must be capable of evaluation with a yes/no answer.

Lastly, how does the prospect take this action?

It is necessary to select a 'shape' for the proposal that will ensure it makes sense to the prospect and can be made persuasive. One that makes sure the proposal will:

- *be well organized,* with the flow of information easy to follow;
- *be put in sequence,* so that the prospect will agree each point progressively;
- *highlight critical areas* of particular interest to the prospect;
- *summarize* all previous agreements;
- state all the facts that the decisionmaker(s) needs;
- *Summarize* all previous agreements;
- *be easily understood*—by all those who may read it;
- *position your organization* in an appropriate role.

There are essentially two approaches, a letter proposal or a formal proposal. A letter is more appropriate to some situations than a formal proposal and vice versa.

In general, the complexity of the sales situation and the prospect's business methods will be a guide to determining which type of proposal to use (see Example 5).

EXAMPLE 5   TWO KINDS OF PROPOSAL FORMAT

Letter Proposal

A letter proposal summarizes the critical elements of the recommendations for the decision maker in a letter. Attachments that document the solution or provide extra information can be added.

The letter proposal is appropriate when:

- A more detailed proposal is not required;
- Recommendations can be clearly presented within the scope of a letter;
- It is necessary only to summarize what has already been agreed upon;
- All prospect concerns are solved;
- There is no competition for the work.

Formal proposal

The formal proposal is a more detailed approach to presenting recommendations. A formal proposal is appropriate when:

- Recommendations are complex;
- Recommendations will be perceived as high in cost;
- The decision maker is dependent upon recommenders and influencers to help make the buying decision and must ensure that their involvement is important;
- The decision maker or some of the recommenders and influencers have not met personally.

Proposal Contents

Each likely section of a proposal is now commented on in sequence:

Introduction

Remember that it is a sales document; the opening must command attention, gain interest and lead into the main text. First impressions are important, so the first sentence must not be wasted.

The introduction may need to establish the background, state the purpose of the letter/proposal, and refer to previous discussions/agreements.

It can also include a title page (with the client's name, an index, terms of reference and credits).

Statement of Need

This describes the scope of the requirement and makes it clear that the writer understands what is necessary, and how it will be decided upon.

Ideally, it does no more than confirm in writing what was originally asked for and added to during the survey visits.

It has the value of emphasizing the identity of views between us, showing the client that we understand what he wants and does not want from an external accountant.

For example, details of client needs for an audit proposal that could be stated individually might include such factors as:

- It complies with existing statutory requirements
- It is unqualified and will satify shareholders when published
- It improves investors' confidence by safeguarding shareholders' interests with an independent viewpoint
- It helps the client get credit from banks and suppliers
- It gives him security by having generally accepted accounting principles giving 'correct' financial information
- It uses control mechanisms proven in his industry, giving him confidence in the production of correct results
- It shares the burden of audit responsibility, by protecting management while also controlling their audit activity
- It allows the situation to be under the client's control at all times
- It gives a minimum of disturbance to his operation and customers
- It does not overload staff
- It avoids the necessity of costly data-banks and in-house experience by ready access to the accountant's skills, especially in tax and accountancy
- It gives information which can be adapted for various user needs, eg, ownership, management and personnel
- It gives cost saving suggestions from familiarity with the organization, eg, systems, taxes etc.

The Solution
This describes the suggestion not just in terms of technical details (features), but in terms of advantages and benefits. If possible, it should be made exclusive, ie, the benefits offered cannot be duplicated by competition.

There is no more effective way to ensure a reader's attention than to ensure that the content of the proposal is totally directed towards him and his needs. Everything which the proposal contains must not only be relevant to the prospect, but its relevance must be explained and he must agree.

A standardized, or unthought out approach, may become confusing or present a programme which hardly refers to what was formerly established, and certainly does not deal in depth with the prospect's real needs one by one.

It is easier to make these points than to determine how they should be phrased. Advantages must be translated so that the implications are apparent, by using a phrase like 'which means that...' Features of the approach, method or services are less important than the benefits – what it means or will do for the prospect. Using these factors together in the sequence benefit – feature will present the most powerful argument, and avoid the comment 'so what?'.

In addition, reference to timings can be made at this stage.

Costs

All costs need to be stated clearly, but related to the benefits of the suggestion, plus any intangible factors.

Quotes must be alive to going rates for similar jobs, and to the prospect's views and perception of fees. The prospect must be convinced that he will get value for money. Since some prospects will only read this section, it should start with a short summary of the benefits of using the firm.

Attempts by the prospect to establish individual scale rates should be resisted if possible, since these may be misleading, particularly if:

- the firm tends to work more quickly and efficiently than others;
- it is usual practice to absorb audit start up costs on the basis of expected recurring examinations.

Even if no fee estimate is given in the proposal, a range or a top figure should be worked out. This is in case of pressure at the presentation meeting, where dissatisfaction may ensue if the prospect receives no indication at all. Do not disguise any costs, but do support them with benefits.

Ethical rules currently forbid getting the job by referring to lower quotes than competitors.

Proceeding to discuss the associated areas of manpower and the implementation timetable may help to move the reader positively away from the costs. It may be useful to amortize costs to illustrate value.

Closing Statement

This can refer to any attachments, for example, literature/samples. It should create a sense of urgency, so that the decision maker will act promptly and should close; ie, ask for the order or commitment, making it clear what the next action is to be.

A summary of why this proposal is right will help those key executives who are very busy and who need a precise statement of the facts to help them make a decision, and those key personnel to whom the proposal was not presented. Repeating the benefits after the costs section means that a reader is left with an impression of benefits not price.

Such a summary might include:

- a review of the origin and scope of research effort;
- an outline of the key findings on what is wanted;
- a summary of what is offered and how that meets the prospect's criteria for external support.

It might finish with a summary of tangible and intangible benefits.

In a formal proposal, each section should have its own page, a table of contents will make it clearer and the letter accompanying the proposal (if it is posted rather than presented) must not be a formality, but should add something to the case – perhaps strengthening urgency or specifying further action, for example:

- It might give appreciation of being asked to work, reassuring the prospect that he was right in contacting the firm;
- It might emphasize that the proposal represents the mutual conclusions of the prospect and the proposer;
- It could close by indicating who can be contacted or promising to contact in the near future, and suggesting a timetable of action.

Style and language are important too. The document should be attractively laid out, gramatically correct and well typed. It should look formal, efficient, individual and clear.

Layout is especially important: it should not be squeezed into one, two or any particular number of pages. Headings and paragraphs will ensure clarity and emphasis; underlining, a PS, or capitals will get the attention wanted.

The intention is to prompt the client to action rather than demonstrate 'Oxford English'. It should be written much as it would be spoken; the following are some useful rules on language:

Be clear	— Make sure the message is straightforward and uncluttered by 'padding'. Use short words and phrases. Avoid jargon.
Be natural	— Do not behave or project yourself differently just because it is in writing.
Be positive	—In tone and emphasis (be helpful).
Be courteous	—Always.
Be efficient	—Project the right image.
Be personal	—Use 'I' – say what *you* will do.
Be appreciative	—Thank you is a good phrase.

Avoid trite openings, for example:
- 'We respectfully acknowledge receipt of...'; or
- 'We have pleasure in attaching...'

If we follow the rules of a good opening, we shall also rarely begin with 'Thank you for your letter of...'

Avoid pomposity, for example:
- 'We beg to advise...'; or
- 'The undersigned/writer...'

Avoid coldness and bad psychology, for example:
- 'Advise/inform';
- 'Desire';
- 'Your complaint/dissatisfaction'; or
- 'Dictated but not read by...'

Avoid cliché endings, for example:
- 'Assuring you of our best attention at all times, we remain...';
- 'Trusting you may be favoured with...'; or
- 'Awaiting a favourable reply...'

Do keep it simple – use short words in preference to long ones; one or two words in preference to several, particularly in the case of those cliché or fashion phrases, like, 'at this moment in time', when we mean now'. These look much worse in print than they sound spoken. Sales checklist number 4 is designed to help in preparing proposals.

Sales checklist number 4

(1) *Have you selected the appropriate proposal format?*

☐ Letter proposal

Yes   *No*

☐   ☐   Can you adequately present your recommendation in a letter with attachments?

☐   ☐   Is it agreed that you need merely summarize what you discussed/agreed?

☐   ☐   Are all prospect concerns resolved?

☐   ☐   Has competition been eliminated?

☐ Formal proposal

☐   ☐   Are your recommendations complex?

☐   ☐   Will your recommendations be perceived as high in cost?

☐   ☐   Do you want to demonstrate the involvement of recommenders and influencers upon whom the decision maker will rely in making the buying decision?

☐   ☐   Will you be unable to meet with the decision maker or with other key recommenders or influencers?

(2) Do you know who may influence the decisions to buy?

☐   ☐   Decision maker?

☐   ☐   Recommenders?

☐   ☐   Influencers?

☐   ☐   Others?   _____

_____

(3) *Does your proposal contain the following?*

☐ Does the Introduction include

☐   ☐   A background statement?

☐   ☐   The purpose of the proposal?

☐   ☐   An emphasis on mutual conclusions?

☐ Does the Statement of Need include

☐   ☐   Clear and specific enumeration of needs directly related to recommendations?

☐ ☐ The scope of the problem?

☐ ☐ A statement of the prospect's decision criteria?

☐ Does the Solution include

☐ ☐ A list of recommendations

☐ ☐ The relationship of recommendations to needs

☐ ☐ A statement of how recommendations meet the prospect's decision criteria?

☐ ☐ The features, advantages and benefits of your products and services?

☐ Does the Cost Statement include

☐ ☐ A summary of the tangible benefits?

☐ ☐ An identification of intangible benefits?

☐ ☐ An amortization of costs where appropriate?

☐ Does the Closing Statement include

☐ ☐ A description of attachments?

☐ ☐ A statement urging prompt and specifically stated action?

☐ Have you included the appropriate attachments/samples?

☐ ☐ Samples?

☐ ☐ Descriptive brochures?

☐ ☐ Others? _____

_____

Comments: _____

_____

_____

_____

_____

_____

_____

_____

Presenting the Proposal

Proposals, however good, can only do so much on their own: they neeed presenting. The evidence is that this happens little at present, particularly among the smaller firms, but it is a growing practice that makes sense for clients as well as accountants – especially if competitors are presenting their offerings.

The moment to agree this, to sell it, is at the end of the survey meeting. Finding out how many copies of the proposal document are needed (which may also provide additional information about decision makers) and setting a date, time and perhaps other details (attendance, location) will allow planning for the meeting that will best help secure the business.

The ability to make effective presentations is an essential executive skill not only in selling to prospects, but also for in-house selling at executive meetings and in making recommendations following an assignment. However, it is an unnatural social act for most people made more difficult by familiarity with a polished television performance.

In addition, many presentations are further complicated by the client trying to follow a proposal while listening to the presenter explaining something different.

The objective of the presentation must be to:

- present the people, clearly and understandably;
- get feedback, avoid monologue and gain agreement;
- present the solution credibly to convince him; and
- handle objections to satisfactorily answer questions and objections.

Using the Proposal

The presenter should prepare his copy of the proposal with notes, examples and headlines to guide his talk. Since competitors will be saying mostly the same things (for example, 'we pride ourselves on our good service'), and because just reading the proposal is not enough, it must be turned into an aid to presentation.

Key elements of the presentation are now commented on in sequence:

Present Clearly

Take a structured lead:

- by suggesting a format and timetable for the meeting, for

example, that you go through the proposal together with discussion after each subject and cut off times in two hours;
- by handing out and briefly showing the contents of the proposal, but suggesting that it will be more productive if you study it together, section by section, starting by ensuring that you have the facts right; and
- by following the proposal and reading aloud parts of it without re-writing it.

Use Prepared Aids
- use prepared aids as visual paragraph markers for ideas;
- keep words to a minimum;
- ensure uniformity of size, colour and layout; and
- introduce the aid, talk it through and remove it.

Use Yourself as a Presentational Aid
- be enthusiastic – if you are not convinced, they will not be;
- stand or sit upright but with varied positions;
- use hands to emphasize rather than distract;
- look at individuals and change expression; and
- vary voice pitch, tone, pace and duration.

Use Language as an Aid to Interest
- use questions as well as statements;
- use metaphors, similes and analogies;
- use examples to paint pictures;
- repeat and summarize frequently before, during and after.

Remember that the proposal is the main aid; it is wasteful to reinvent the wheel.

Get Feedback, Avoid Monologue

Know your 'man':
Money
Authority
Need

Choose a Style of Delivery
- Will you address the decision maker or the audience in general?
- Will you use a formal stand up or low key discussion style?
- Will there be a greater or lesser involvement of a team?
- Will there be a liberal or selective use of aids?
- Will you make use of customer language/jargon?

Check for feedback by continually involving the prospects, to

get their agreement before moving on. Getting them nodding early on, refer to the situation, to matters clearly agreed.
- Watch faces and body movements for reactions;
- Ask questions to ensure agreement on the need to introduce each main point;
- Do not move on if people are still worried;
- Summarize frequently;
- Make notes of points of agreement and disagreement; and
- Watch the time.

Present Credibly

The presentation is the occasion when the prospect and his team are able to judge the human side of your suggestions.

He will be using the opportunity to assess your complete capability for:
- doing what you have said;
- doing it better than competitors;
- integrating with his own staff; and
- not causing extra work or problems.

You must pick your team and agree roles, so that there is no confusion during the meeting. Deciding exactly who goes from your side, and how many, is important, as is the link between that and who will do the work.

Give proof:
- Build up the team's credibility;
- Demonstrate *how* your firm has been successful;
- Allow individual experience to shine (without boasting);
- Use expressions like 'in our experience...';
- Work in examples of how you have worked in the prospect's industry;
- Illustrate your arguments with published references;
- Quote convictions and agreements already made by the prospect; and
- Above all, talk throughout in terms of benefits.

Experience of having successfully worked in a company like his is often what the prospect is looking for; if you do not have it how close do you come?
- Ensure that the decision maker and all his advisers are present.
- Ensure that they are pre-sold and looking forward to your presentation.

- Avoid presenting anything new that may create resistance.
- Emphasize the points that have already been agreed with the decision maker and his advisers.
- Reinforce your message with simple, graphic visuals.

Proposals represent the summation of the effort with the prospective client, and the commitment to him. This does not mean that large amounts of information should be submitted just to look impressive, but it does mean that it should be carefully thought out and well organized.

A well prepared and presented proposal increases client confidence, essential when selling accountancy services, and increases the possibility of success.

The need for formal presentation at this stage, what some firms call 'the beauty parade', is increasing as clients become more and more inclined to check out any appointment very carefully. It is a key element in differentiating one firm from another, and one that may demand some training within the firm. One practical aid to this process is the training package *Making Competitive Presentations* which my own company, Marketing Improvements, produced in collaboration with BBC Milton Keynes. This provides a way of developing skills within the firm using a comprehensive set of manuals, video, audio and other materials, and is specific to selling professional services (yes, it is a plug – I am enough of a salesman at heart to allow myself one blatant one in a whole book!)

Persistence and Follow-Up

Many a job has been lost by default because of poor follow-up. Accurate follow-up is always necessary to correct misunderstandings, carry out promised actions and to show keenness for the client's business. After each call, building goodwill, making the client feel it was a worthwhile contact, even if his commitment was not made, it is a valuable investment in the future. Follow-up action should be automatic, and made immediately after each call while ideas are fresh. A record of what was promised should be made as a prompt to the next action. It may take conscious effort to make sure that the logistics of the business allow the follow-up that is necessary; 'production' responsibilities have to be phased in with selling.

Similarly, once the business is booked, the process does not stop. With existing clients every meeting should be regarded as a potential opportunity to identify new work possibilities, sow the seeds for new projects or propose new projects or propose new work.

Sell *on*   – offering new, different services to what has already been done;

Sell *up*   – increase the value of existing work and extend the scale of involvement;

Sell *across* – the other parts of the client company (subsidiaries, locations, etc).

Seek reference to other sources of work and, of course, simply repeat what you have done (next year's audit).

'Time is money' is an old cliché, but sales effort and client contact of the sort described take time. The more certainly it is done, the better the conversion from opportunity or prospect to firm business, the greater will be the impact on profitability. (See Chapter 7.)

Some of the skills involved may not be thought of as the accountant's primary stock in trade. Competitive pressures are steadily making the point that the accountant must make them so or feel the lack of them in the future. This is especially true of selling.

Chapter 7

Client Development

**'Life is what happens while you
are making other plans'**
John Lennon

Client Development is certainly among the most discussed topics at partner level in many firms. But while the concept of client development is often accepted as necessary and desirable, precisely how this process can best be initiated, managed and controlled within the firm's overall business and marketing plan, remains a largely unsignposted trail.

As an example, one firm where I presented this idea to their annual partners' conference felt this was an idea with real merit and left committed to action. A year later, asked what progress had been made, the senior partner reported that they 'had had three meetings to discuss exactly what sort of system should be instigated'. But no action. We all know the feeling.

So the specific objectives of this chapter are to provide appropriate and implementable guidelines – 'signposts' – in this key area. As a result of this, it should be possible to form clear links between the overall marketing planning process described in Chapter 2, and the activities and control processes necessary to translate marketing strategy into action in respect of client development.

Before going further, client development should be defined; it is the management of client relationships in such a way as to hold existing business, maximize the likelihood of identifying opportunities for further work and progressing them to the point of agreement for more work to be done. It is an ongoing process and an additional dimension to the management of client work, not an alternative to it.

The Marketing Role of Client Developement

Links to Marketing Objectives and Strategy

Any firm approaching the implementation of a client development programme must recognize that the preceding stage – evaluation of clearly defined overall marketing objectives and strategy choices by the partners in the firm – must be done *first*. The planning forms 3-12 in Chapter 2 provide the minimum desirable overall planning framework for the firm. If notes are recorded under these headings, this will provide the necessary coherent framework of reference, within which client development activities can take place. By adopting this systematic approach the firm can make optimal use of the key resources of time and money; and ensure its ultimate selection of which market segments and which 'development opportunity clients' form the potential market, from which profitable growth can most likely be achieved.

Marketing Objectives Reviewed

In that they have deep significance to the evolution and implementation of the client development process, the six major marketing objectives available to a firm are worthy of a brief review. They are:

- *To increase market share*
  In a static or low incremental demand market this can only be done by 'conquest' selling – that is, winning business from other firms.

- *To expand existing markets*
  This involves focusing on selling the fullest range of the total service portfolio to existing clients. It also implies that very close cooperation and communication must exist, or be fostered, between those working on, for instance, compliance work and those working on other services.

- *To develop new services for existing markets*
  This can involve either the revision ('re-packaging') of existing services and/or the introduction of completely new services. This is one of the growth routes already adopted by many larger firms, who have progressively added needed services to their 'historic' service offerings, eg the addition of computer services, specialist consultancy on production management, distribution analysis, etc.

- *To develop new markets for existing services*
  Given the statutory nature of audit/compliance work in the UK this option is increasingly limited. By its very coverage, statutory legislation has identified all major potential users. However, an expanded service base in more specialized offerings can offer clients the opportunity to test at first

hand the fundamental competence of a new potential supplier of audit services. This has meant that additional, if more fundamental, business can be won by a progression from a 'service portfolio expansion' approach.

- *To develop new services in new markets*
  This is an example of true diversification and, as the highest risk marketing objective, has been traditionally eschewed by many firms. Competitive pressures and the need to retain good staff by offering high 'challenge' and personal development opportunities may force a review of this attitude in future.

- *To improve the profitability of existing operations*
  In mature markets, where little incremental demand exists, many firms must, in the short term at least, seek higher returns from greater productivity and cost-efficiency of their operations. It is perhaps self-apparent that if firms have pursued this route to the ultimate and profitability still remains at less than satisfactory level – then more 'offensive' marketing objectives are called for. These are the only logical alternative to business shrinkage resulting from static or declining profitability.

The Link To Promotional Activity

The plethora of promotional activity forms an earlier part of this book. In terms of client development, and whatever permutation of marketing objectives are selected and pursued, promotional activity divides into two main areas:

(i) Marketing communications
In the broadest sense, the primary objectives of all marketing communication, ie advertising, public relations, seminars, etc, are (a) to create an enquiry or 'opportunity to do business' with new clients and/or (b) to remind existing clients of additional services on offer from the firm and/or (c) to reinforce continuing usage of existing services. No matter which of these primary objectives are set for the various elements of the communications mix, only face-to-face selling will ultimately determine whether or not marketing objectives are actually realized.

(ii) Face-to-face selling
The primary focus of all promotional activity is face-to-face

selling, which is the most appropriate, relevant and effective form of promotion for any firm offering professional services. By definition, professional services are people intensive, the people are the product, and must form the final link in the promotional chain.

Attitudes to Client Development

The greatest opportunities for profitable business development lie in building from the existing client base. Like any promotional activity within the profession, it must be conducted ethically and, perhaps even more important, in a manner that is acceptable to clients – otherwise any effect will be wasted. But, in this respect, an opportunity only exists when all members of the firm working on existing assignments with clients are organized, prepared, and equipped to *look for it!*

The only situation in which such opportunities can subsequently be pursued, prioritized and capitalized on, is through personal contact with client decision makers and influencers.

If opportunities are not to go by default, then it is vital that *all* members of the firm from individual accountants to managers and partners share the attitude that, in working for, and communicating with existing clients, *two* priorities exist:

(i) To perform to the highest technical standard on current work, so that a client re-books that similar work with the existing firm as their supplier, wherever that type of project is required on a 'repeat' basis.

but also

(ii) That this should go together with 'opportunity search' ie the planned identification of *current* needs which are not being met by the firm, or its competitors, and changes in the client's market environment or operating or organizational policies which will give rise to *new* needs, which can be satisfied either by existing services, or the extension/ development of services within the firm's capabilities.

Why Are Client Development Opportunities Missed?

Opportunities *are* missed! In which firm can it be objectively said that an opportunity has *never* been missed; that no client has brought in somebody else to do something you *could* have done?

The reasons include:

(i) Over reaction to adopting a 'selling' stance.
(ii) Lack of insight that 'opportunity search' is a vital activity.
(iii) Lack of awareness of other services which the firm offers. (Often despite a firm conviction within the firm that everyone knows clearly everything in the range of services!)
(iv) Lack of persuasive communicative skills.
(v) Focusing on the 'urgent' (today's tasks) to the exclusion of the 'important' (creation of tomorrow's business).
(vi) Lack of clarity on the firm's business development needs.
(vii) Lack of a coherent sales development plan for existing clients within the framework of clear overall business development objectives.

Managing The Client Development Process – Overview

Although all are important reasons perhaps areas (vi) and (vii) are the fundamental causes and areas (i) to (v) are the resultant effects in relation to the key question – why are opportunities missed? Conversely, this argues that a systematic framework for managing the client development process must be followed. A suggested staging for this is:

STAGE 1 Develop and communicate clear overall marketing objectives and strategies specifically in relation to business growth.

STAGE 2 Decide *where* in market segment and client terms these objectives could be met.

STAGE 3 Develop/initiate a thorough review of the existing client base to highlight where opportunities may exist (situation analysis).

STAGE 4 Decide where clear opportunities *do* exist (account development strategies).

STAGE 5 Focus attention on client development priorities through evolution of specific sales plans.

STAGE 6 Allocate specific priorities to individuals working on current client assignments. (*Who* does *what* by *when*.)

STAGE 7 Evaluate and control the development process over the plan period.

STAGE 8   Analyse where significant variances in planned vs. actual performance lie.

STAGE 9   Take corrective action where and when necessary.

STAGE 10 Feedback results and experience gained into the *next* marketing plan.

Initiating the Client Development Process

So far, we have referred at several points to the importance of the management of the client development process taking place as a planned element of the overall marketing plan. We now turn to the key questions, and resultant specific approaches and formats which are necessary to implement the client development *management* process, at stages 3–10 in the systematic approach outlined above.

Organisation

KEY QUESTION 1 – HOW WELL ARE WE ORGANIZED IN RELATION TO CLIENT DEVELOPMENT?

Where Do Responsibilities Lie?

One of the key organizational problems to be solved in a firm offering professional services and operating with the objective of growing the practice through client development is how the appropriate amount of the 'production' and 'sales' resources can be put behind each function.

The 'production' and 'sales' resources tend to be the same people and this becomes a more difficult problem in the smaller firm where, overall, there are less people.

In most firms, client development is regarded as *everyone's* responsibility. If this approach were to be adopted in a 'raw' state, or applied literally rather than systematicaly, the only predictable result would be, at best, unplanned client development and, at worst, utter chaos.

In the early stages of business development, therefore, the responsibilities can best be clarified by considering the overall client development process in three component parts, namely:

(i) The overall *marketing planning work* such as data

collection on markets, analysis and decisions on objectives and strategies and construction and communication of overall plans and systems.

Because of the objective and policy forming nature of these activities, some firms have successfully allocated this area to a 'practice development' partner. He, as it were, wears 'the marketing hat' and while he may not personally do everything, has a key role in initiating and controlling activity.

In most firms, the success of this overall part of the client development process depends heavily on the goodwill, insight and frequency of communication between senior members of this firm. This is particularly vital if marketing objectives of developing additional business via increased/new services to existing clients are being pursued and if the audit practice is separated from the other main services. Forms 3–12 in Chapter 2 provide a review of the range of planning documents likely to be useful, within this area of responsibility.

(ii) *The implementation work* – the 'selling-on' activities in relation to existing and new clients which must be carried out by the whole firm within the framework of the overall marketing objectives. Because of the increasing range of services offered, some firms have set up 'project teams' for the largest existing or potential clients to provide the full range of skills and experience necessary to make progress and ultimately to satisfy client needs.

At an overall planning and implementation level two factors seem to aid success. First, that responsibility should be concentrated rather than spread. Thus if a new service is to be successfully launched and subsequently grown within, say, the existing client base, it is more effective to commit an individual or small group to that action. As a result, *internal* publicity or 'knowledge-building' about the service itself and its potential benefits to clients can be most effectively pursued. From this process, *external* 'applications' (markets and target clients) can most readily be identified. Implementation then rests with those staff who have the greatest knowledge of, and the best relationships with, the decision makers in the 'target' clients for the new service.

Secondly, that the development activities are, wherever possible, defined, quantified and timed at the planning stage. However, this definition must specify the links between the results required and the development activities or clients.

(iii) *Translation* of the two preceding marketing planning processes into specific account (client development) plans. In this context 'account plans' are the quantified and qualified client-based action programmes through which the firms' overall marketing objectives will be ultimately achieved. Precise guidelines and formats which clarify and exemplify the account planning process are dealt with in subsequent sections.

Responsibilities Beyond Development of Current Client Opportunities

Beyond the development from the *current* client base, responsibilities will need to be allocated in relation to new/prospective clients who are the by-product of either:

- referrals from existing clients;
- enquiries resulting from marketing communication activities, ie advertising, PR, seminars etc;
- previous clients who have not used the firm's services for some considerable period of time.

In general terms *ultimate* responsibility for turning enquiries into sales will always rest with senior partners. There are several factors which necessitate this, namely:

(i) By nature of their management role in the *total* practice development process they are inherently in the best position to examine whether the potential assignment:

- provides an acceptable 'fit' between the current or planned services offered by the firm and the client's requirements;
- they are in the best position to forward the enquiry to other senior managers into whose discipline area the potential project may fall, if it is *not* their own.

(ii) Being involved in the initial stage allows them to check later whether the new business enquiry resulted in subsequent fee income.

(iii) They should also be in the best position to judge whether specific individuals have the technical competence, selling skills and *time available* to rigorously and efficiently pursue the most potentially desirable business opportunities.

In practice, many firms adopt a systematic allocation of responsibilities, where *initial* vetting and any necessary qualification of an enquiry coming into the firm by letter or telephone is done by senior partners, and at the earliest possible stage the enquiry is then delegated to the individual at 'operating' level who can best pursue it. While delegation of that pursuing should be to one person, on whom responsibility for making sure it happens rests, this does not mean that others will not be involved in the follow up process. Sometimes 'team' selling is necessary and appropriate. Senior partners should remember the difference between 'managing' an account and 'directing' it. A background role may be important and will always include acting as backstop to make sure sales opportunities are not missed.

Enquiry Progress Form

An enquiry is a crucial starting point from which new business can result either from prospects or new clients. Such contacts are too important to be allowed to go by default. A form, perhaps one you design (or adapt) specifically for your firm or even your department, bestows an importance on the enquiry. It should act first as a record; with copies being passed on as necessary (not least to build up the information you need for ratio analysis). Second, it acts as a checklist; to prompt whoever is taking the enquiry to ask the right questions. Items like the job title of an enquirer, important to help ascertain where he is in the decision making hierarchy; or whether and by whom he was referred to you, useful to evaluate promotional activity, may easily be overlooked.

Last, and by no means least, such a form can be used to ensure an enquiry is progressed promptly and efficiently; specifying and recording action. The last entry on such a section should always be the next action you decide upon. While it may not always be possible, indeed necessary, to complete all the form, everything beyond the basic information may help, that is, it may increase the chances of a sale ultimately being made successfully.

A reference number can be used to tie in with other systems within the firm.

Such a form can either be designed solely to record the enquiry – as in Form 1 – or linked to subsequent stages documenting:

- Details of initial enquiry;
- Subsequent action;
- Result for the firm – as in Form 2.

In both cases NCR-type carbon sets of form facilitate communication.

Continuing Sales Attention

Earlier the key organizational problem of deciding how the 'production' versus 'sales' resources could best be organized and committed was referred to. Often these responsibilities are vested in the same individual, and line reporting relationships and the nature and flow of the day to day workload can either facilitate or impede the effective allocation of effort necessary to develop business while performing current assignments to the highest standards.

As with so much of marketing there is no magic formula, but two main approaches are being adopted in firms providing professional services to help alleviate this potential dilemma.

The first, referred to previously, is that where *new* services are introduced with the initial objective of selling these into existing clients, specific responsibilities for building *internal* awareness of the service and *external* client opportunities for it rest with an individual or a small group. Outside of the profession, this relates closely in principle to the 'brand or product management' function found particularly in consumer goods organizations.

It has the essential merit of pre-selecting the appropriate service for its correct client market, in relation to overall marketing strategies.

Secondly, 'relationship management' principles (about which, much of the remainder of this chapter is concerned) with their ongoing review of client reactions to completed work, and resultant or emergent opportunities, are an inherent part of the client development/assessment process over time. This process can be most appropriately undertaken by the staff directly involved with the client, who also initiate contact with more senior personnel or other specialists as and where appropriate. It is also evident that in some firms at least, efforts are being

Form 1

	ENQUIRY PROGRESS FORM
To:	
Ref No: From:	

Enquiry taken by: Date:	Company:
	Address:
Source of enquiry:	
Stated need:	Tel. No:
	Contact name:
	Position:
Comments:	Nature of client:
	Additional information:
Action taken:	
Action promised (inc timing)	

Subsequent progress:

Date	

	Resulting Fee	Value	Date
		Job Number	

Form 2

BOOKED/REFUSED

Date:

Description of assignment:

Company Name:

_____

Value [ ]

_____

Location [ ]

_____

Ind Class [ ]

_____

Work Type [ ]

Job No [ ]

| Refusal reasons: | | Staged Booking Amount o/s [ ] |

Price [ ]   Reproposed [ ]

Other Ref Nos _____

Competition [ ]   Age [ ]

Client A/c [ ]

Other _____

Engagement Partner
(project manager)

PROPOSAL

Description of Work:

Company Name:

_____

Location	

_____

_____

Value £

_____

_____

Ind Class [ ]   Group

_____

Work Type [ ]

_____

New Client   Yes/No

ENQUIRY PROGRESS FORM

Source of Enquiry [ ]

Advertising [ ]   Existing Client [ ]

Company: _____

Public Relations [ ]   Personal Contact [ ]

Centres of Influence [ ]   Seminars [ ]

Address _____

From: _____   Via Associates [ ]

_____

Referral [ ]   From: _____

_____

From: _____

Tel No

Other _____

Stated need: _____

Contact name:

_____

Position:

_____

Industrial Classification:

ACTION: BY WHOM _____

Comment:

BY WHEN _____

made to move *beyond* historic 'blind alleys'. For example, a management letter which only reflects areas historically audited, but goes no further to highlight or examine current or potential needs for additional professional services which the firm can provide, is allowing opportunities to go by default. Appendices to the management letter, an agenda for client review meetings which prompt discussion on future needs, etc, are effective methods of cost-effectively moving transitionally from 'today's assignment' to 'tomorrow's business development'. Ensuring the thinking exists which produces this degree of fine-tuning of actions in a way that makes them an integral part of client development is crucial in any firm.

Information Systems

KEY QUESTION 2 – DO OUR CLIENT INFORMATION SYSTEMS HELP THE BUSINESS DEVELOPMENT PROCESS?

Information Systems – Overview

Client information systems in many firms are limited to a simple historic database listing clients' addresses, contact names and similar primary details, recorded either on client files, individual record cards or, increasingly, in computer systems. In many cases, important though it is in its own right, this information deals only with the direct operating information specific to a particular project, ie contacts at senior and line level, within the financial organization/division of the client firm.

However, for any firm seeking business growth through client development, three critical areas will need to be examined:

(i) Do existing records give sufficient qualitative depth, so as to aid *future* business development opportunities, rather than simply provide a *past* record of work done?

(ii) Do the information systems themselves provide to the firm as a whole, sufficient depth of information to avoid 'reinventing the wheel' by being able to access historical projects similar to the one being addressed, thereby reducing the work involved in new client assignments and/ or give insight to relevant service related solutions?

(iii) Do they aid the business development process by providing cross-market or cross-disciplinary links to enable the firm to highlight industry trends and issues? This will help prepare 'state of the art' business advice and informed new business presentations, to either existing or new clients, which demonstrate reasonable understanding of the issues which the client is facing in his markets.

While no panacea or generally applicable solution to these questions would appear to exist – providing all things to all firms – certain implications are clear, namely:

- using client information systems in a purely historic context;
- collecting and recording *narrow* assignment-related information;
- storing information in a manner which is difficult to access;

will not, of itself, provide *any* direct help to the business and its client development process.

If systems are to provide a real basis for client development, comparison of what is *currently* known about clients with what specifically *needs* to be known to opportunity spot now or in the future – a 'gap' analysis – forms a logical starting point. This type of analysis should be conducted at two levels within the firm. First, by senior partners as a integral part of the marketing planning process, and secondly by assignment managers in relation to specific clients, particularly at the opportunity search stage of account planning.

What Information is Needed?

Collecting data and organizing it is a most challenging task which requires both good judgement and sound method. Good client files are the most critical element for sound planning. In this context – 'knowledge is power'.

Specifically, the following information should be available on 'priority' clients:

(i) General/historical
- History of their company
- Ownership
- Subsidiaries, if any
- Organization structure
- Corporate objectives
- Problem areas – current
- Problem areas – potential
- Financial status

(ii) Financial data
- Profit and loss, balance sheet data
- Key financial ratios
- Comparisons of ratios on an inter-firm, inter-industry basis
- Credit worthiness
- Payment history, etc

(iii) Marketing data
- Client's key markets and trends, evolution, etc
- Competitors active in his markets
- Profiles of buyers, influencers, etc in his markets
- Product range/width/depth
- Future market/product plans
- Distribution routes
- Pricing policies
- Communications activities
- Sales force organization/methods
- Market position
- Market share
- Environmental factors likely to affect his markets
- Legislation affecting his operation

(iv) Competitive data
- Which other professional service firms do they, or have they, used?

(v) How decisions are made on professional services
- Who decides?
- Who influences?
- The decision-making process
- The basis on which decisions are made
- The time scales involved

(vi) Key contacts
- Names
- Titles
- Ages
- Needs:
   –personal
   –job
   –departmental/others.

- Ability to buy
- Authority to buy

- Best time to meet
- Attitude:
    - –constructive
    - –supportive
    - –positive
    - –critical.

Sources of Information

The above information will clearly, in the main, be built up and added to as the needs and priorities for business development clarify over time. But whether for an initial, or subsequent 'developmental' or review meeting with a prospective or existing client a sound base of up to date information is crucial to credibility. Any client can lose faith in uninformed suppliers, quite apart from any personal insult they may feel.

Background knowledge also provides a supplier, particularly of professional services, with another most precious commodity – personal confidence. This communicates itself to clients and builds credibility. In this context, the following sources are worthy of consideration:

- colleagues/senior partners/client records and files
- local/trade/national press
- industry/trade shows and seminars
- directories/yearbooks/agencies:
    - Jordan Dataquest
    - Intercompany Comparisons Ltd
    - Financial Times Yearbook
    - Dunn and Bradstreet
    - Who Owns Whom
    - The Directory of Directors
    - Kompass
    - Investment Houses
    - Economic Intelligence Unit
    - Local Authorities
    - Chambers of Commerce

- the prospect/client himself:
    - Annual report
    - Share prospectus
    - Internal PR publications
    - Organization charts
    - Industry contacts

This information building process does not just happen – it must be planned and reviewed regularly. The above list is essentially illustrative and there are other sources of information which can be tapped with a bit of research, effort and creativity.

Storing and Retrieving Client Information

Based on the numerous information needs and sources available, the problem is less one of acquiring information than how, by who and where it should be recorded and accessed.

A useful start point is to divide information into two broad categories:

(i) Operational information – which will be needed by staff working on current assignments, business development projects, etc. As, by its nature, this type of information will tend to be used at 'point of contact', ie on client's premises, it needs to be:

- concise, eg Kardex or A4 size;
- coded, rather than explicit, in confidential areas;
- secure at all times.

(ii) Long term or strategic information – which will be needed by staff working at the firm's offices, will tend to be more permanent and comprehensive in nature than operational information. By its nature this will include correspondence, annual account plans, proposals, reports, client background information, etc.

Increasingly many firms are regarding much of this information as transposable where appropriate onto computerized record systems. Clearly, policies must be established so that while information is accessible for sales planning and development purposes – it is also secure from unauthorized or unnecessary access.

By its nature this is a decision area which cannot be generalized – every firm must make its own decision to fit its specific environment and priorities. Some firms in professional services are tackling at least some of the inherent problems mentioned by establishing a third client information base, namely:

(iii) A job-experience database – the primary objective here, beyond issues of security versus accessibility, is to provide the cross-industry, cross-discipline information links referred to earlier (in Information system - overview). This is particularly relevant in professional firms where:

- previous/contemporary industry knowledge and experience can be a key 'differentiating' factor in winning or growing business in a competitive climate.
- 're-inventing the wheel' may occur. For everyone this can have a potentially costly effect on time spent and fees lost or incurred when on any assignment new methods and approaches are developed from scratch, rather than on the basis of what has been previously done or originated. If a good starting point is missed a job may immediately become less profitable.
- trends at an industry level need to be monitored by senior partners in an 'opportunity search' client development context.

The Job/Experience Database Form shown illustrates an input/summary which is equally applicable to manual or computer-based systems. Clearly a master-file or index would need to be added to ensure overview and access. In large firms with regional offices linked by computer it can be accessed from several points.

Categories of information held might include:

- Work type classifications
- Project/job codes
- Industry sector
- Industry code
- Client name
- Summary of what was done
- Problems encountered
- New approaches used/material developed
- Relevance to other companies/industries

This approach has the additional merit of providing 'core' information at a number of stages of the marketing planning/account planning process and can also be cross-referenced back to original enquiry/progress forms of the type illustrated earlier.

This summary provides the end-view or *'review'* stage of progress with specific clients to a total process which started with a *'preview'* at an enquiry stage.

Fundamental Client Information Principles

In conclusion two principles are worthy of restatement:

Form 3

JOB/EXPERIENCE DATABASE FORM

JOB REF:

CLIENT:

NATURE OF ASSIGNMENT:

VALUE:

STAFFING:

SUMMARY OF WHAT WAS DONE:

PARTICULAR PROBLEMS ENCOUNTERED:

NEW APPROACHES USED OR MATERIAL DEVELOPED:

RELEVANCE TO OTHER COMPANIES/INDUSTRIES:

(i) 'Gap Analysis' – measuring the difference between the information *available* vs. information *needed* is a key first step to making information bases future orientated, ie focused business development, rather than passively *historic*.

(ii) The problem with information of this type is potentially one of 'overload' – given multiple requirements and sources – rather than 'shortfall' – but the decisions on how, where and with whom this information is stored and how it can best be accessed, must be addressed and answered.

It has been said, with some truth that 'if your system works well, it is obsolete' so constant review is necessary to refine and develop the agreed system, and make sure it remains relevant to current operations.

Without this systematic approach, today's excellent system will inevitably deteriorate into a future 'filing system' or archive.

New Business Selection

KEY QUESTION 3 – CAN WE CLEARLY AND OBJECTIVELY SELECT NEW BUSINESS OPPORTUNITIES?

New Business Opportunities – Overview

Though the prime concern of client development is by definition with existing, known, clients these must originate somewhere and before moving on this section looks at how new business originates.

There are three fundamental routes by which new business is created or 'arrives' in the client portfolio of a professional firm, namely:

- building business in existing clients (developmentally);
- enquiries from potential clients (reactively);
- solicitation of business from potential clients (pro-actively).

As previously discussed, the first two rely essentially on selling skills, ie seeking and capitalizing on opportunities to expand business from the current base and handling new enquiries from the initial to commitment phase efficiently and effectively. The latter, third, new business route is essentially a 'pro-active' rather than developmental or reactive method. At the time of writing, the ICA guidelines on solicitation of business clearly define what is, and is not, permitted promotionally. All methods of marketing communications ie advertising, PR seminar, etc will be the fundamental method by which totally new clients can be accessed. Given that the ultimate objective of marketing communications is to create an 'opportunity to do business', ie an enquiry, this will then fit into the second area *or* route by which new business can ethically be created and progressed.

But, irrespective of the route taken, certain fundamental principles apply to new business selection. As far as possible it should be *planned activity,* should be subject to *vetting* of specific opportunities at a relatively senior level and should be a *controlled* process. This latter principle is patently a by-product of the first two.

The search of new business opportunities should be planned so that:

- opportunity stimulus exists, preferably on a regular, phased, basis;
- future opportunities (market sectors, professional service areas, specific clients) are examined and assessed for development at the planning stage, wherever possible;
- guidelines and definitions of what constitutes desirable and acceptable *new* business are established and *communicated* as an integral part of making the firm's plan known to anybody involved in the next period's client development process. This will avoid time wasting advances in directions not fitting with the firm's overall plans.

and *vetted* so that:

- any new business opportunity of significance, in fee terms, can be assessed against the firm's plan and how it would utilize resources;
- the 'fit' with the firm's overall objectives and strategies can be assessed;
- the opportunity cost of pursuing an unpredicted opportunity against planned client or market development can be evaluated;
- trends can be assessed in the new business area;

and *controlled* so that:

- resources and effort remain focused on activities within the scope of the original plan.

(It is accepted that all of these steps are based on an, arguably, optimistic scenario, in which sufficient opportunities exist from which to select. But to ensure that this state does *prevail* is, after all, the purpose of this chapter as a whole.)

It is without doubt worth re-emphasizing that new business selection and review is made much more systematic and objective and much less 'hit and miss' if a solid business plan – and marketing plan – exist in the first place. A review of the business/marketing planning process is largely the subject of Chapter 2.

Selecting Worthwhile Potential Clients – Currently and In The Future

Using the preceding overview as a 'thinking frame' is the first essential step. However, there are specific questions which must be posed, discussed (and answered!) and criteria set within each firm as follows:

- Overall, do we *know* what constitutes a 'worthwhile' new client?

and more explicitly

- Do we know if it is really likely that a particular prospective new client will agree to buy a significant amount of our services, measured in fee income, either now or in the future?

- Have we the resources to cost-effectively meet his needs?

- Does the nature of his need, or the complexity of his business require a major investment of time/staff available?

- Can the scale/rate of likely fees be cost-justified to him?

- Does this client's 'buying history' (with you or other professional firms) imply a significant opportunity?

- Would gaining this client create a desirable knock-on effect in his or other industry/market sectors – is it a prestigious and influential account to have? (Beware – judgements here must be very pragmatic.)

- Will the cost of the 'inputs' in time, staff, work load, terms be significantly less than the 'output' in revenue terms?

- If not, will the costs involved in gaining experience here be immediately recoverable by creating opportunities for the firm elsewhere in the market?

- Does this prospective client/enquiry offer significantly

higher opportunity than other prospective business currently under review?

- Do we have the services which he needs currently available?

- If not, how urgent is his need? And if it is not urgent – but a *major* opportunity exists – should we develop our capability to meet his need?

No such list of selection criteria can ever be exhaustive – but these questions represent the 'filter' questions posed by many professional firms. Equally, not all of them can be answered instantly – often further qualification with a client, and/or a period of internal discussion is necessary. Both of these steps – when needed – are vital, if only to avoid accepting or rejecting business opportunities without due consideration. Equally the review process should not take too long – even the most desperate client has limits to his patience! This means for establishing filter or vetting standards at an early, rather than a later stage in the business planning process.

Strategically, two questions should *always* be asked when a significant opportunity exists:

- Does this opportunity conform to our current strategic plan?

- If not, is pursuing and accepting it strategically justifiable?

It is self-evident that these two questions can, and should, only be finally answered with decisions at a senior level within any firm.

The Link With Promotional Activity

In selecting new opportunities, there are two main links with promotional activity, the first 'causative' and the second 'preventative':

- The *causative* link assumes that all promotional activities – whether by marketing communications or personal selling effort, are targeted effectively, and that key business development areas have been segmented realistically.

  Further, that correct methods of promotion – non-personal or personal – have been identified and used within the context of the *total* communications 'mix' available, and that the service 'offer' matches the promotional objectives, in type and benefit.

- The *'preventative'* link assumes that resources and action are subsequently committed only to opportunities produced by promotional activity, ie in the market *segments* identified in the original promotional plan.

This has two implications – *first* by its nature it is a way of measuring promotional activity by *results*, against objectives, rather than cost or expenditure committed or incurred. And *secondly* the source of any enquiries which happened by 'accident' rather than by 'design' can be examined to see whether more effort or expenditure on promotional activity in that area can turn 'accident' positively into 'design'.

A good example here is at least one professional services firm who now systematically use public seminars as a promotional route, among other purposes, because of new business which arrived originally by 'accident' from this source.

Establishing Client Relationships

KEY QUESTION 4 – HAVE WE CLEARLY IDENTIFIED THE <u>RELATIONSHIPS WANTED</u> WITH, AND BY, KEY DEVELOPMENT ACCOUNTS?

Establishing and Management of Client Relationships

Not only is the market environment characterized by high competition, but the work of professional service firms is, at least in some areas, being perceived as 'commodities' by clients, (eg compliance work). With performance standards which are in many cases percieved by clients as 'technically' the same whoever may supply professional help, establishing and maintaining *positive* client relationships can provide a key 'differentiation' opportunity for many firms. In this context a firm's most precious assets are its *relationships* with its potential or existing clients.

There is little doubt that decision makers mentally position potential and existing suppliers of *all* services and products within a spectrum which might be represented as follows:

CLIENT PERCEPTION TOTALLY NEGATIVE	CLIENT PERCEPTION TOTALLY POSITIVE

├──┼──────────────────────┼──┤

Expressed Attitudes	*Expressed Attitudes*
'They're only interested in fees'	'They're interested in our total business'
'Simply another supplier'	'They stand out from other suppliers'
'No different than the rest'	'They are different-positively!

While this obviously represents an extremely polarized view of client perceptions and attitudes it highlights the truth of the old saying 'You don't have to be different to be good, often being good is different enough'.

Differentiation is critical and is less a matter of gimmicks than efficient and creative client orientation. Specifically, therefore, the following points on relationships are important:

- *Positive* relationships based on mutual trust, credible performance and good relationship management by supplier firms will inevitably win more business at the potential sales stage, and preserve more business at post sales stage.

AND:

- *Negative* relationships where mutual trust is lacking, performance appears at best average and poor relationship management exists will inevitably not win business at the potential sales stage, and most certainly cause the client to ask competitor firms to propose for the current supplier's business.

It is axiomatic that most firms will want to be positioned positively rather than negatively in this 'perceptive' area. But, as with other areas of the client development process, it won't just happen – these relationships must be planned, managed and reviewed constantly, by *all* staff who have contact, developmentally or operationally, within client companies. Maintenance and enhancements of client relationships do not so much depend on an annual lunch with a senior partner, good manners, public relations, charm, diplomacy, window dressing and manipulation – rather on the insight that:

- Any relationship with a client can, perhaps inevitably will, decay over time.

- Managing the relationship progressively and consistently is much more effective, than trying to pull a neglected relationship back from the edge of the abyss down which the client's fees are about to disappear! Attention to client relationships is akin to preventative maintenance on a car.

In a demanding, and increasingly competitive professional environment, technical competence *alone* is clearly no longer enough – creating a sense of mutuality, growing the *business partnership* is a vital extra dimension.

Benefits of Well Managed Client/Accountant Relationships

Truly effective client/accountant relationships where high trust and solid relations exist, pay off in two key ways:

- The *work* performed can usually be done with less inherent obstacles in the way – in the sense that information, comments or support from the client and his staff are without doubt given more readily and willingly to someone regarded as a 'working partner' than to a perceived 'third-party accountant'.

- The *sales* process – gaining further work where the client needs it, adding services which are of true value to the client, or repeating regular assignments – is inherently easier. Any of us talk more openly about present problems, other needs we have, where priorities may change in the future and so on – to people we trust and have a mutual relationship with, than with somebody who is simply 'doing their job'. Referrals to other clients are also more readily given to somebody who is valued beyond simply their technical competence.

Managing Client/Accountant Relationships – Practical Steps

Managing the client accountant relationship implies conscious actions to control and expand the 'account', a process of 'selling-on'.

This process involves three stages:

- Establishing the relationship
- Managing the relationship
- Reviewing the relationship.

Establishing the relationship – starts at meetings preceding the 'sale' of a project. The process here is built on pre-meeting research. Prepared information can make it clear to the client that knowledge and interest in his industry and business are important to you; and using such information as a base to discuss in depth where *his* problems, needs and priorities really lie and then basing subsequent proposals on his *priorities* enhances the relationship at this stage. The first meeting represents a significant opportunity to begin to stand out from the crowd.

Selling techniques deployed at this stage should and can enhance the building of a relationship and in fact provide the first opportunity with a new contact to demonstrate professional competence. In other words, the way selling is conducted should be instrumental in positioning the firm and individuals in the right role for the future.

Managing the relationship – can be effected in a number of ways, some of which may appear obvious, but are worth re-emphasizing:

- Send 'thank you' letters on client acceptance of assignments;
  - to emphasize the time which the client has previously committed to you in the decision-making stage,
  - to reinforce the implementation of the project,
  - to maintain a sense of mutual urgency.
- Ensure that any project is proceeding in the way that both parties agreed;
  - to ensure it is on time,
  - to ensure it is within cost parameters,
  - to prevent frustration or dissatisfaction,
  - to pre-handle any problems or complaints,
  - to turn 'promises' into 'realities',
  - ideally checking at prearranged review points.

- Monitor and report the *results* of your actions/activities;
  - to keep the initiative,
  - to create new opportunities,
  - to keep in contact with the decision maker(s),
  - to re-emphasize the *benefits* of your work to the client.
- Expand your contacts in the client firm;
  - to increase awareness of his total activity,
  - to brief, where ethical, other executives on past/present activities and benefits to them.

- Keep *au fait* with the client's industry and business;
  - to help you identify other recommendations,
  - to confirm the client's confidence in you as an interested and informed 'business partner'.

- Read the clients's publications;
  - to identify additional client priorities or needs.

- Try to attend internal meetings of key clients;
  - to present your services on subjects under discussion,
  - to keep clients informed of any of the firm's activities which might be of interest.

- Invite the client, or his staff where appropriate, to your functions;
  - to cement the relationship.

- Try to get involvement in the client's planning processes;
  - to advise objectively where emerging priorities from his side coincide with developing services from yours.

- Establish a key client monitoring system;
  - to record past and current activities,
  - to plan future activities together.

If you find that such actions have no benefit, or seem inappropriate to you or the client's business, you will obviously think twice before carrying on with them, but many of them do have positive value in building and growing the client/accountant relationship. Other ideas must be created to keep the process fresh longer term.

A form is useful to decide/plan what steps should be implemented – and what the results over time have been, in the relationship management process. While it is unlikely that every one of these actions should (or can) be actioned with every client with equal emphasis, assessing the value and impact of them is a key stage from which many firms will potentially benefit. It is a good idea to make sure there is on every client file a document that records sales action taken and which, like the enquiry form, ends with the next action that it is intended to take in order to progress the business. Once such action has led to a specific request to discuss some particular project being made then the enquiry procedure can take over.

The intentions of such a form are again to act as a *record*, a *checklist* and *prompt*.

It is not possible to specify how these forms should appear in every firm or department. However, Forms 4 and 5 are examples of two which are intended to act as blueprints from which other, more individual, forms can be developed.

Whatever combination is selected, one of the most effective methods for 'selling-on', which is the ultimate objective of relationship management, is to conduct formal, timely reviews with the client's senior management.

Reviewing the relationship starts by researching, through discussions with colleagues or staff involved, or in discussions with client staff, results obtained by them from current or previous work. During such activities identify satisfaction levels, results obtained by the client firm, other priorities and problems – and thus highlight any *new* requirements. A process of collating these findings, discussing priorities with the key client contact and other interested parties, getting their current 'view of the world' and presenting further recommendations at a *formal* review can now be made mutually productive. In some firms this is already an adopted process, following or during *internal* reviews of current or completed projects.

Formal client review meetings will be at their most productive if structured along lines such as these:

- Review and compare achievements of the past period.
  - original objectives set,
  - solutions proposed,
  - work undertaken and completed,
  - benefits obtained by the client,
  - discrepancies, if any, between objectives and results with reasons.

- Present new proposals;
  - needs and priorities which currently the client has,
  - solutions, ie ways you can help,
  - benefits and results which the client will receive.

- Present an implementation programme;
  - objectives,
  - actions and milestones,
  - review points.

- Gain commitment from the client to the next step.

Working systematically in this way has the potential to both check relationships and client perspectives and perceptions, turning new clients into retained clients, retained clients into

Form 4

To	From:
Ref No.	**CLIENT REVIEW FORM**

Work being carried out:	Client:
	Address:
	Tel No:
Project manager:	Contacts: Name Position
	1.
	2.
Completion date:	3.
	Type of organization:

Follow-up sales action:

Date	

Work proposed: Value £

☐ Agreed   ☐ Refused – Reason

Form 5

RELATIONSHIP MANAGEMENT PROGRAMME

CLIENT .... PERIOD ....

POSITIVE ACTIVITY PLANNED	R/E*	BY WHOM?	WITH WHOM?	WHEN OR FREQUENCY (IF APPLICABLE)

*Regular or Exceptional?

Key Points – Why this strategy and activity?

_____

Success Criteria	Results

The Accountant's Guide to Practice Promotion

growing clients and, therefore, aids in making time invested on client development activities most productive.

Relationship Management Reviewed

It is realistic to emphasize here that not all clients – and not all professional projects – require the same degree of relationship cultivating and effort. These decisions are judgmental and will be different, even by degree, for every firm. However, *whatever* effort and investment is made in cultivating the client/ accountant relationship, it should be made in a systematic and regular way. This means that any firm interested in *developing* client business must be sensitive and alert to the risks involved in simply letting relationships evolve by *laissez-faire*. Opportunities can too easily go by default, and competition is increasingly vigilant.

For a client, agreeing to do business with a firm offering professional services is only a *first* step. How the total relationship develops after this point, as well as pure technical performance, affects deeply his decisions 'next time around'!

'Business partners', if that is his perception, rather than 'simply another accountant', are valued and retained, rather than easily substituted or replaced. Being seen as a 'business partner' is dependent on good relationship management. Just hitting it off well with the client is no longer likely to be sufficient.

Planning and Executing Client Development Strategies

KEY QUESTION 5 – HOW WELL DO WE <u>PLAN</u> AND <u>EXECUTE</u> CLIENT DEVELOPMENT STRATEGIES?

Planning at the Client Level

At several stages so far it has been emphasized that, even assuming a clear commitment to the principles of client development, 'it doesn't just happen – it must be planned'.

But it is also worth stressing that planning – and executing the plan, ie making it happen – can't take place in a vacuum. By its very nature and because of its critical importance – new business creation via coherent client development strategies must be a

202

part of an integrated and complete process:
Integrated in three directions

- *'Downwards'*, in that an overall business and marketing plan must first exist, if only so that client planning in relation to business development, has a corporate framework in which to operate.
- *'Upwards'* in that, if reasoned new business development plans at the client level are generated at the right stage, they become an 'input' at the formative stage of the firm's overall business plan, ie an estimate of potential from existing clients forms a key part of forecasted business growth.
- *'Sideways'* in that, at a time when firms are expanding their involvement in additional disciplines and thus the 'service portfolio' on offer and, at the same time expanding geographically in many cases, ie new offices or special divisions for taxation, management consultancy, etc – client development plans should, by their nature account for the *total* business development potential for that client on a cross-discipline, cross-geography, etc basis. 'Sideways' integration alone provides a superb communicational/ opportunistic basis on which individuals in different disciplines and/or different locations can cooperate and 'synergize' on business development opportunity searching and knowledge sharing. This is possible because there is a *common* core on which the plan centres – the client, rather than the technical discipline involved.

This background provides the basis on which the key question of *'how* well do we plan and execute client development strategies?' can, at the first stage at least, be answered, ie is it objectively an integrated process:

- downwards?
- upwards?
- sideways?

If the answer is yes – senior partners should still ensure that it continues. Integration of planning is, frankly, challenging and time-intensive – better to restress internally from time to time the inherent benefits than to have to act as a 'doctor to an ailing patient' if integration is decaying.

If the answer is no – consider the risks inherent in 'planning in a vacuum'. Even the best overall business plan is not capable of operation if client development activity 'on the ground' is not happening. Conversely the best client plan can ultimately become a form of 'guerilla warfare', if it is working in spite of, or at cross-purposes to, the overall business plan. This can cause potential irritation or lost opportunity across disciplines, offices geographically separated, etc. Many firms have learned these lessons the hard way, but those with clear, integrated plans for client development now have an advantage over those operating on a more *ad hoc* basis.

For Which Clients Should Detailed Developments Plans be Developed?

The purist would say – 'every single one'. The realist would say – 'if that is possible – certainly', but in practice 'prepare *detailed* (and that is the key word) plans for, at the very least, all major clients'.

If the realist's view is to be adopted then definitions of major/key/developmental clients are called for; these clients are those which:

- produce high volumes of business or potential,
- require a high level of attention or commitment of the firm's staff, at all levels,
- have possibly high potential for other services which the firm can provide.

Additional 'indications' are that they exhibit some or all of the following characteristics:

- any one client that accounts for in excess of, say, 5 per cent of the firm's overall business, measured on a time/fees basis for each of the firm's services;
- clients whose level of business with the firm is such that losing it would have significant effects on the firm;
- clients who have an obvious potential to grow to these levels of business and importance;
- clients who are major opinion-formers (and therefore affect other client relationships).

How Do Such Clients Differ from Other Clients?

In practice the answer here will vary from firm to firm but some indications are:

- they require a lot more attention through visits, etc;
- they provide the opportunity for larger potential sales, and more risk;
- in dealing with them, the firm will tend to be in a more

'competitive' situation (and the client knows it!);
- more decision-makers or influencers;
- more chance of the firm coming up against organizational politics;
- the decision-making process can be complex;
- the firm will have to maintain *overall* client satisfaction, ie in several departments or divisions;
- more and better information will be required.

In other words they are different not just in size but in nature, and most emphatically therefore more detailed client planning will be required for them.

Detailed Planning for Major Clients

It has already been made clear that plans at the client level are extremely important – the real implication of what has been said previously here is that the client plan forms the 'operational dovetail' to the strategic business plan of the total firm.

Because it can be a time-intensive process, there is still evidence in the profession, and indeed in the wider business world beyond that, of resistance to a client planning process in detailed form. Two frequent areas of critical comment can be summarized in statements like these:

'The more detailed it is – the more it operates as a strait-jacket to us.'

'Developing our business is essentially *opportunistic* – unpredictable events cause additional needs which we can meet and therefore, why write a predictive plan for something that can't be foretold?'

These comments are understandable. But, on being stated they contain, paradoxically, the very answer to the comments: that substituting the words 'defined parameters' for 'straitjacket' emphasizes the need to define the logical limits within which development activity can freely take place – without conflict with the firm's overall plan.

Business development is, to no small degree, 'opportunistic'. But planned activity, if it includes true insight into what may happen in the client's own markets and operations for the next year(s), centres on ensuring that predicted changes in his needs or priorities, are, wherever possible, linked to timely and logical action plans. Not least this ensures that our presence is felt as a 'business partner' as and when the changes occur. Thus the plan beings together opportunity and action on the planner's part and to his, and the client's mutual benefit. As was indicated earlier opportunities only exist when they are seen to be, and they coincide with solutions a professional service can provide.

A well reasoned client plan ensures that people, money, time and support facilities are used to best advantage. This is of vital importance in obtaining business from major clients, since more often than not a team of people will be involved. Without a detailed plan the problem of coordinating their activity would be considerably greater. In addition, without a plan it is difficult to ensure that the correct priorities are allocated or that minor, but still important, aspects of the firm's activities are not overlooked.

Planning – Not Just Plans!

Dwight D Eisenhower – who was responsible in 1944 for the biggest movement in history of men and material once said:

'Plans are nothing; planning is everything'

The important thing which Eisenhower highlighted was that a fixed, rigid plan was useless in itself; the important aspect was the planning process. This covers analysis, forecasting, objective setting, strategizing and programming.

The client plan, which is of course concerned with the future, must be flexible in its construction so that it is able to adapt to changes, since the future cannot be predicted with a high degree of accuracy. Thus a plan defined from forecasts is useless if it is seen as a set of actions which must happen. The planning process is as important as the plan which should in any case be more like a route map than details of one road.

Formalized Approaches to Client Planning

A formal plan serves as a framework for day-to-day decision-making and provides a method for follow-up and evaluation of how client development activity is progressing.

The planning process should supply answers to the following questions:
- Where are we now? (Analysis);
- Where are we heading? (Trend analysis, forecasting);
- Where do we want to go? (Objective setting);
- What is the gap? (That can or must be filled);
- How do we get there? (Strategic and action plans);

- How are we progressing? (Controls).

The answer to the last question (monitoring actual results against the planned results) is, of course, an input to the others over time. In practice any good planning process is always continuous.

Planning consists of four distinct phases:

(i) Where are we now?
Where are we heading?
This phase is concerned with a situation analysis – a process of putting together the history of the performance of all services, market climate etc and the identification of future opportunities and threats and present strengths and weaknesses within each major/key client.

(ii) Where do we want to go?
This phase encompasses:

- Assumptions – those conditions in the client firm or market which cannot be quantified and for which we have to assume a certain posture.
- Statement of objectives – these are the goals which have been identified for the client plan and should be quantified specifically in areas of,
  - value/mix of professional services
  - share of business
  - profit, where the directive of fee income less attributed costs can be deducted.

(iii) What is the gap?
How do we get there?

This phase encompasses:

- Basic strategy – defines the specific approaches we will take (major courses of action) to achieve the objectives of the plan.
- Specific actions – these will define:
  - *what* needs to be done (detailed actions)
  - *when* it needs to be undertaken and completed by
  - *who* is responsible for those activities?
  - where appropriate, the *costs* of that

activity, eg notional or fee cost of a senior partner's involvement.

(iv) How are we progressing?

This phase addresses itself to the controls and review procedures – these are the mechanisms for monitoring actual performance against planned performance and initiating corrective action when things do not go according to plan.

The client plan is a formal statement of the support effort for a *specific* client. Developing the plan involves the following steps:

- Situation analysis of the client company
  - opportunity and threats identification,
  - strengths and weaknesses analysis.

- Objectives within this client situation
  - including assumptions about those conditions which cannot be quantified.

- Strategy statement
  - encompassing the main strategic actions to be pursued.

- Actions plans
  - including costs or budgets for the activity where appropriate,
  - timescales for the activity,
  - support required.

- Control and review procedures
  - with other firm's personnel, 'internally',
  - with the client, ie formal 'external reviews'.

FIRST STEP – SITUATION ANALYSIS

The first major section of the plan is an examination of the present situation – our 'trading performance' with the client and the present and future business environments in which both the client and therefore, you as suppliers of professional services, are operating. The situation analysis section itself can be usefully divided into four sections – an account profile, normal forecast, opportunities and threats and strengths and weaknesses analysis. This encourages a *systematic* situation appraisal by the person responsible for originating the plan.

Section 1 – the client profile

This sets out a profile of the client company showing:

(i) Your present business volumes, expressed as fee income, and services used;

(ii) Your present share of the business by service and 'usage' area;

(iii) A description of the trend by service and 'usage' areas;

(iv) A cost analysis identifying all costs directly incurred in dealing with the client, eg attributable promotional/ support costs, personal cost estimates against fees generated, fees attributable as costs of other's time, etc.

A quantitative analysis of the particular client will now exist, in terms of fees/usage by service or service groups, and the relative costs incurred, together with a picture of trends and some indication of share of customer business in relevant service areas.

Section 2 – normal forecast

The client profile should be followed by a forecast of the firm's 'sales' to this client under 'normal conditions'. This is what might occur assuming no major changes in the marketing environment or marketing strategies of the firm.

Clearly the preparation of this forecast requires close liaison within the firm at a senior level, and reference to client records of past activity. Detailed client knowledge, ie from the uniform client information/research base (see Information systems discussed earlier) is essential.

The forecast would have to be revised if quite different environmental conditions are expected or strategies are planned, eg economic growth, legislation, competition and changes in the firm's or this client's activity.

The current and probably future 'sales' picture will now exist. However, the picture is a forecast and not yet necessarily agreed targets or objectives. It is the answer to 'where are we heading?'.

Section 3 – opportunities and threats identification

The normal forecast section should be followed by a section in which the person developing the plan identifies the main opportunities and threats facing his firm.

The opportunities and threats describe outside factors facing the client and supplier of professional services, ie the firm. They are written so as to suggest possible actions that might, by implication, be warranted.

The main opportunities and threats for the future are likely to be identified from the following areas:

Economic factors, if it is, say, an industrial client, – will *his* markets grow or decline? – if he is exporting, will exchange rates, import quotas changing, etc affect his business, financially or organizationally? And, as a result – will such factors affect his needs for our services, thus limiting or expanding the *use* of our services?

Technological factors/changes, eg a client entering a market for computer systems may need additional services in business planning, the raising of venture capital, additional management accounting systems. As a corollary, a client whose business may be eroded by a competitor entering his market with a substitute or replacement product may need management consultancy services, or – at worst – assistance from our insolvency colleagues!

Political/legal factors, eg effects on the client of likely changes in, say, product liability legislation, which will affect *his* products detrimentally – he may need additional help in inventory management, etc.

These are simply intended to illustrate what *analysis* of opportunities and threats can provide if used as a 'thinking frame'. With major/key clients in volatile markets, or who are organizationally complex, discussion and sharing of views with colleagues within the firm can be a useful and desirable process. This is 'sideways' 'downwards' and 'upward' integration in its most practical and potentially potent form!

As the above examples illustrate, an *opportunity* only exists for the firm if it can be met either with the expansion of a service currently used or the use of an additional service, within the firm's current or planned portfolio.

Because of this, it must be relevant to follow and dovetail the opportunity/threat analysis with a strengths/weaknesses analysis. It is only then that a changing future situation for this client can be truly categorized as opportunity, threat, or simply a future event which has no effect for us – or is someone else's opportunity!

Section 4 – strengths and weaknesses analysis

In this section of the plan the quality of the firm's offering to the client is evaluated. This will enable the value to both parties to be determined. As a result an extra dimension is added to the quantitative picture of 'sales' and profit, which will be required to determine an effective strategy to achieve the objectives.

A simple format is to divide the firm's offering into three main component parts:

(i) 'Product' – services
(ii) Fees and terms
(iii) 'Presentation' and support

and assess them against the *competition* in each of the areas of the client's operation where a buying influence exists. Again, good knowledge is required – of client buying influences and needs, and of competition (generally and *vis-à-vis* this client).

Step 1 in the strengths and weaknesses analysis would be:

Service analysis
The depth of detail will vary from service to service (or range) and client to client but the aim is to identify strengths and weaknesses *vis-à-vis* competition *as seen from the client's point of view*, using a concept of value analysis.

Step 2 would cover:

Fees and terms
A similar exercise should be carried out for fees and terms. In looking at fees, the supplier should be aware that his service will be of varying importance to different clients, and different areas of his operation will be viewed differently (not only fees but the total terms of business should be compared).

This is becoming an area in which many firms are benefitting from a market-based approach to fees charged and, indeed, what fee levels are tolerable ie 'sensitive' or 'insensitive' in the *client's* view. For example audit fees may be a 'market sensitive' area, ie a client may turn to other firms if fees appear to rise dramatically in relative terms, to say, last year or those charged by others. On the other hand, fees charged for say the origination of Inventory Management Systems, which bring stock costs dramatically down or ensure they are kept under control, may be perceived as tremendously high in *value* by the client. In such cases relatively higher fees may well be perfectly acceptable.

Step 3 would cover:

Presentation analysis

The term presentation is used to refer to all the other factors associated with the supplier's offering besides the service itself and fee levels/policies.

Examine all the elements of support provided to or *needed by the client* and compare your standards against competition *as seen from the client's needs*. This will include such things as:

- advice on legislative changes;
- specialist seminars on topics such as personal taxation;
- seminars of an *ad-hoc* nature, ie budget briefings, etc;
- the firm's links with *intermediaries;* solicitors, banks, management consultants, market research firms, etc;
- documentation, ie standard business forms;
- access to specialists or senior partners, overseas offices of the firm, etc;

The Steps Following a Situation Analysis – the Client Plan Itself

Client plans will vary in depth or requirement, formats which are most suitable and *degree* of precision needed, from one firm to another.

This notwithstanding, some explicit guidelines on the client plan generation process, terminology and areas of potential difficulty would be useful, if only to establish a framework for discussion within your firm. (Experienced planners may choose to skip this part – but why not review it anyway – experience itself can change over time!)

Ingredients of a Client Plan

Given that situation analysis is a pre-cursor and will provide detailed insight into the 'forward situation' the firm will face, plans subsequently generated should have the following *three* ingredients:

- *Objectives* – which are essentially end results in key areas. These should be as clear and concise as possible and should concentrate specifically on what the firm expects to *achieve* with this client in the plan period. General or modifying remarks that fail to further define the objectives should be avoided.

A useful 'acid test' is to ask whether the objectives are 'SMART', that is:

Specific —stating *precisely what* will be achieved by the plan, evident in a form that is:

Measurable —that is control area performance standards, etc can be applied where required (see Control and evaluation discussed later in this chapter).

Achievable —within the resources available?

Realistic —fitting the overall business plan of the firm (essentially *'should* we be doing this?' – as opposed to 'can we *achieve* it?')

Timed —specifying how effort and support is spread effectively throughout the year's client activity, times/dates exist for key activities, and that deadlines or review points exist?

- *Strategies* – which essentially define the 'route' which activity will take. Stategy is the vital *link* between objectives and action programmes, the frame into which activity fits.

  Strategies should concentrate on those major elements of the programme which will be directly responsible for enabling the firm to achieve its desired goals. Statements should not go into minute detail about the activity in question. These are covered in the plan of execution or 'tactics'.

- *Action programmes* – which essentially define the detailed steps necessary, in pursuing. Precise detail on *who* does *what* by *when* are needed here.

  Action programmes are, by nature, *tactical* – they define the 'week to week' events by which the *strategy* with the client will be followed, in order to achieve the stated *objectives*.

Special Techniques

Detailed and comprehensive client planning may involve certain special techniques, for example the following:

Statistical Forecasting – specifically in answering the question 'Where are we heading?' (trend analysis). This is essentially the mathematical extrapolation of past sales figures into the future on the assumption that all the variables will remain the same.

Sensitivity Analysis – specifically in the area of defining scientifically likely reactions to fee levels, etc. This is often causally linked to the overall technique of 'value analysis'.

Specialist help should be sought if these two, and indeed, other techniques are used, where the firm's, or indeed the planner's own, knowledge is less than required.

The Client Planning Process Reviewed

The overall development of major client plans should be an annual process and involves the following:

- Forecasting 'sales' and profit objectives;
- analysing strengths and weaknesses of the firm's 'offering' in the client's eyes;
- developing a major client strategy;
- identifying the main activities to be carried out to ensure that the objectives are achieved.

Unless meaningful plans are drawn up, the activity towards key developmental clients will tend to become uncoordinated and the results are likely to be less successful. Experience shows that those firms who carry out this planning activity most effectively mobilize their resources more efficiently, are more likely to maximize the revenues and profits they achieve and have a more mutually rewarding relationship with their major customers.

For the plans to make maximum impact they should be:

- specific, listing detailed activity;
- easily measured, quantified wherever possible;
- succinct, easily read and understood;
- directive, showing clearly what is required from each individual (or department) concerned;

- a basis for commitment by the individuals involved to achievement of the objectives.

The Link To Records/Systems

In addition to guidelines given earlier – Information systems – some comments on how client development plans, and planning, link to records/information are worth mentioning.

Because detailed client plans are 'information intensive' – a tremendous amount of factual data needs to be reviewed, fed into or generated at the planning stage – information gathering should be done over time. Those who have to suddenly find the often detailed information required when 'the plan' is due (or late) will appreciate this point. As an adjunct to this, it is clearly valuable to have record systems which both record factual data over time – progressing as and when it is collected and provide the information easily – in the form needed – at the planning stage.

Several firms, through insight or 'remembered pain', have made client planning systems essentially 'rolling' plans and formats, ie details of what has been achieved, costs involved, opportunity/threat analysis, etc is regularly reviewed and updated throughout the year. This has four effects:

- The client plan and record systems at client level are automatically linked, and the format/content of both can be reviewed together.
- The client plan is under progressive review during its operational stage.
- The 'state of affairs' shown in the client record is always firmly up to date.
- The *next year's* plan – particularly in the information area – takes far *less* time, in that a minimum of 're-inventing the wheel' is called for (or finding out from scratch where the spokes of the wheel have been buried!)

Involving The Client In The Process

Client development should not be viewed as something 'done to' the client in isolation. Involving the client in the process makes sense from two major directions – philosophically and practically.

Philosophically because it is after all not simply our future as a supplier we are planning, it is the client's too. If professional services are going to have an impact on his future, perhaps his input is desirable.

Practically because a client may well have gone, or be going through a similar planning process – and, therefore, have readily to hand data or views on his markets, financial requirements, opportunities, etc. Consider the potential time to be saved if we can tap into his views and plans for the future. The planning stage also provides a superb opportunity to review with major clients the year gone and the period ahead. In this sense, it is a logical point for formal review, at which future links may be formed and is a tremendous 'opportunity generator'. Mutual planning discussions also help forge, or re-forge, the 'business partners' approach described in the section regarding relationships.

Control and Evaluation

KEY QUESTION 6 – DO WE EFFECTIVELY <u>CONTROL</u> <u>AND EVALUATE</u> CLIENT DEVELOPMENT ACTIVITY, IN RELATION TO THE OVERALL BUSINESS PLAN?

Making Sure the Client Development Process Takes Place

Detailed planning for major/key clients must be, by its impact on client development activity, an exhaustive process. Particularly if being done for a number of clients for the first time in depth it can be, as many can readily confirm personally – an exhausting process – both physically and mentally!

As with all major endeavours, once the planning process has been completed, there is an understandable tendency to sit back and 'relax a while'. And here is the point at which many a good intent starts to go wrong. Planning is the *first* step – actions as planned, *must* follow – or the whole process will become an irrelevant and costly 'theoretical exercise'. This is worth considering in particular if first steps are being taken in this area, perhaps initiated by the marketing partner. If a lot of effort is expended to no good effect, then the credibility of all such activity will take a knock. It may therefore be worth linking first steps to fewer, really key clients, where certainty of follow through should ensure results and set the scene for increased activity thereafter.

The purpose of control, the point of evaluation, is to ensure first that what has been planned is happening and secondly what is happening is being compared to the original plan.

The by-product of control and evaluation is to make the planning process dynamic. This will ensure it is happening, and consistently feed into the client planning system fresh information to keep both the plan and the client information ('data') bank as up to date as is necessary.

This process, as a *dynamic* one, can be pictured thus:

3 INFORMATION FLOW

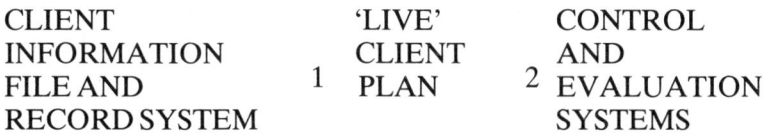

CLIENT INFORMATION FILE AND RECORD SYSTEM		'LIVE' CLIENT PLAN		CONTROL AND EVALUATION SYSTEMS
	1		2	

At point 1 – The client information file and record systems provide *data* for the client plan.

At point 2– What is happening *during* the plan's 'operational' phase is being assessed.

At point 3 – The results of control and evaluation are being fed back as 'updates' to the client information system and record file, which *itself* provides an accurate base on which the next plan is written. And so on.

This, at a glance, emphasizes the *positive,* as opposed to the very common, punitive nature of the control process. Frankly, it is a fundamental insight which is often overlooked. More philosophically, controls are a 'friendly policeman' rather than a 'sentencing judge'. The ultimate purpose is to ensure that efficiency (required results) are never overtaken, in a hectic life, by effort in the wrong direction.

Methods of Control and Evaluation

Applied methods for control will vary in their precise nature from firm to firm particularly in the detail required in planning. This detail, as a judgement area, should itself include definitions of the details of control points in the client development process, but several guideline points can be usefully made, in terms of the nature of controls in the client development process.

Some key questions to ask, follow these initial points:

First, the control process is the assessment by 'variance

analysis' of whether key performance standards are being met, ie the formula:

Actual result – Standard = ± Variance

(To accountants this is fundamental ground of course.)

In this context, it is answering the question posed earlier (in relation to the client planning process: 'How are we progressing?).

This of course reinforces the fact that for control to be possible performance standards have to be stated in the initial plan.

Secondly, controls provide guidance through feedback on how well the individual responsible for the actual achievement of the planned client development process is performing. On a broader front, they also provide those *managing* the personnel working on client development activities with explicit feedback on how well they are motivating 'their people'. In most firms success is a cooperative effort and the results of this, positive or negative, can be pragmatically measured here. This itself suggests that future resources in management support, additional promotional expenditure, training, etc can be committed more objectively, through a two stage process of:

- Measuring *what* has happened;
- Asking/discussing 'why?' if significant negative variances exist.

Thirdly, control and evaluative standards can be of three distinct types, all of which are inherent in a well thought through process, namely:

'*Absolute' standards* – such as total revenue produced by the year end from the client, total costs attributable, total attributable profit, revenue producing hours spent, non-revenue producing time spent, etc. These types of 'absolute' standards have a primary strong point in their favour – they provide just that, an 'absolute' measurement of what *has* happened. These results serve as the 'facts' – the prime standards achieved (or not, as the case may be). But these types of standards also have an inherent weak point – history cannot be changed! They measure what *has* happened, but it is then usually far too late to redress any negative balance – except in the future, for example, via next year's plan. Absolute standards alone or predominantly applied, are inherently risky in the critical area of client development activity/plans.

'Moving standards' – provide a more useful standards basis. If client development results are monitored by those managing the activity, on a monthly, weekly (or sometimes even daily) basis, variances can be identified more readily and trends in the variances will allow future problems to be predicted and, where the right corrective action is possible, avoided. For example, client A's plan might call for a project following an audit to be agreed 'sold-in' by October latest, so that work could commence in November. But if this does not happen because the person responsible has been tied up on an overrun project at client B, then either '(i) someone else could be sent, if suitable, to talk with client A' ; '(ii) someone else could be sent to release the person tied up at client B'; or (iii) if there is no someone else – at the very least, it will be known that the estimated fees from client A are in jeopardy'. In which case plans need to be laid showing how to 'replace' this revenue some other way.

This example, if lengthy, also makes a further point, in that 'moving' standards can be further refined if a third type of standard is applied.

'Diagnostic' standards – can help identify why performance is varying from plan and are defined by asking the question 'what affects the achievement of success?'. For the person managing those responsible for client development work, these are particularly useful, in identifying the actions that staff themselves must take, which, in turn, lead to achievement of objectives set. Fundamentally there are only four, in relation to 'sales' activity for professional service, namely:

- What clients are staff meeting on development 'calls'? Are these the right ones, or kinds?
- How many clients are the subject of specific development 'calls'? Are these as against plan, in numbers terms?
- Is contact *frequency* appropriate? Are we staying in touch, as and when opportunities predicted arise?
- What is actually done by staff, in a face-to-face development 'call' with clients?

All of which can be summarized as 'Are we as a firm, and as individuals, doing the *right things*, at the *right time*, at the *right frequency*, with the *right clients* to ensure our business grows according to plan?' *This is the essential link which binds client development activity to the business plan for the firm as a whole.* This argues for one more repetition of our basic theme that 'client development won't just happen − it must be planned'. Control is an essential part of this process.

The following checklist of key control questions may prompt internal discussion:

(i) Have we defined the key areas of activity that need to be evaluated?

(ii) Have we defined what is 'success' in each area?

(iii) Have we identified the factors that will affect success in each area?

(iv) Have we established appropriate criteria for evaluating environmental, client and the firm's performance?

(v) Do we know the sequence of likely causes?

(vi) Does our information system provide data to compare against the success criteria?

(vii) Do we have a systematic approach to variance production analysis and corrective action?

These answers can provide a powerful guide to the *quality* of existing plans, at the firm's and at each major client's level. If there are no answers, or the answers are unsatisfactory, then action is necessary sooner rather than later. The only alternative is to leave client development, and thus the growth of the firm, exposed as a hostage to fortune in the hostile and increasingly competitive market for professional services.

Guidelines on Client Development

In the early stages of this chapter six key questions were proposed to those in firms concerned with *managing* the client development process. They bear repeating here on *two* counts:

- First, addressing these questions is fundamental to making the challenging process of client development a *planned* process, rather than just *hoping* or *expecting* that it will happen.

- Secondly, on the grounds that there will be at least one reader who will travel by the least lengthy route from start to finish, that is, from the opening paragraph, to this summary, without dwelling or glancing too deeply at the intervening thousands of words. For *that* reader, – if any of the following questions provide a moment's disquiet in terms of the quality of *your* answer to them — go back and read the guidelines in that area at least. If client development is important to your future, and your answers give you pause for thought, haven't you just added one more element of potential risk to what is an already challenging future for the profession as a whole?

The six key questions are these:

(i) How well are we organized in relation to client development?

(ii) Do our client information systems help the business development process?

(iii) Can we clearly and objectively select new business opportunities?

(iv) Have we clearly identified the *relationships wanted* with, and by, key development accounts?

(v) How well do we *plan* and *execute* client development strategies?

(vi) Do we effectively *control* and *evaluate* client development activity, in relation to the overall business plan?

Looking to the future there is little doubt that the profession faces an increasingly hostile and competitive market environment, from a numer of directions. Competition from 'within' the profession is intensifying. Especially the large firms are taking a much more overt, 'pro-active' approach to business growth – adding more services to their existing portfolios, for example. This is probably a powerful route to growth – by creating client experience and satisfaction with the experience.

This, combined with many clients' wishes to reduce, rather than increase their suppliers in numbers, means that other firms providing more limited services are, by definition, under increased scrutiny by the client, and increasing competition as a result.

In addition, competition from 'without', ie the work being undertaken by banks, management consultants and specialists is growing in scale and nature in that these organizations are also reacting to fierce competitive pressures in their own more traditional markets. Their route to growth increasingly overlaps what was once the exclusive preserve of the Chartered Accountant. Professional ethics and standards are, by their nature, there to ensure that the client doesn't suffer in this process, but underlying attitudes to what constitutes a legitimate target, within these ethical standards, are certainly changing.

Thirdly, clients are becoming more demanding and, as many firms will bear witness, are no longer content to view services such as audit on a 'sitting tenancy' basis – clients *will* shop around, *will* demand value for money in terms of that often ill-defined 'something extra'. Clients are also more aware of what other professional firms offer, both qualitatively and quantitatively.

For many firms, this scenario means that repeat business, or business just walking in the door, is not an automatic process. Existing business has to be defended, and new business has to be won. That is the future and whether that leaves the reader feeling besieged or encouraged is the most telling point of all. For those firms who have planned the development, who are ensuring that it happens the future looks pretty good from where they sit. Albeit that there is always an element of risk – planning and execution of carefully considered client development at least reduces the risk to an acceptable minimum.

The process here described should not be rejected as overkill. It will take time. Particularly first time round, but not a disproportionate time in terms of the size of business provided by major clients, the potential inherent in them and, perhaps even more important the impact of losing them.

It is too easy with the pressures that exist on time to ignore or shortcut the process, and perhaps other elements of marketing also, the implementation of which would add a new dimension to a firm's growth. As Beatle John Lennon put it 'Life is what happens while you are making other plans'. The danger is that direct competitors are not so complacent, take more of an initiative and reap the benefits. A final word reflects a repeating theme of this book.

Client development is a vital part of the marketing process that contributes directly to a firm's success. It must be planned, and controlled. It will not just happen, it demands initiation. That is a challenge and a marvellous opportunity. These guidelines are designed to help in a small way to make client development contribute to at least some professional firms' futures – and thus to their planned business *growth*.

The Planning Process

As has already been said, client development should only take place within the context of a defined, agreed and documented plan for the practice. How such a plan is put together is something that was documented in detail in Chapter 1. The intention of such a process is not that a disproportionate time should be spent creating paperwork. It is however, important that the plan is formal and in a form that can be circulated to all those involved. Preparing it will clearly take longer the first time, if no such document exists; thereafter it will be easier and, in part, will only need updating.

The forms that appear in Chapter 1 represent a useful checklist of the headings under which information should be compiled and, for many firms, also a guide to the amount of information that caň usefully be captured.

They are included here to enable this process to be revisited so that client development can be pursued in context. For example, it will help ensure services that may be appropriate for a client to fit the firm's strategy, that new work will meet the pricing strategy for the period, and that other promotional activity planned for the period will fit appropriately with more personal action being taken with individual clients. Once the planning process is grasped, it should progressively take on the form of an action plan and help prompt the whole process. Only then is the danger of securing more business, from more clients, increased.

Afterword – The Future

'Well done is better
than well said'

Benjamin Franklin

There was a time when no detailed understanding of marketing was necessary in accountancy. Indeed no use of most of the techniques it involves was permitted.

Time, and an increasingly competitive environment, have changed all this. Accountants have moved from an awareness of marketing, to an understanding and acceptance of the need for it. Many are now struggling to get to grips with the techniques which are involved and now permitted. This implies a broad range of activity; assessing what services to offer; taking a marketing view of fee levels; experimenting with sales techniques – and coordinating the complex range of activity that makes up the promotional 'mix'.

More and more have discovered that initiating activity in these areas provides real opportunity to increase practice growth, development and profitability. Some are proving very good at it, in some cases to no-one's greater surprise than their own.

Of course responses, attitudes, and results vary, but one factor I would venture to suggest is common. Everyone has discovered there is more to it than meets the eye. Marketing does not come in the form of 'magic dust', a quick sprinkle and the practice grows and develops. Would that it were that simple! Understanding of many techniques and the coordination of them is essential, and it takes time. However obvious, this cannot be overstressed. Implementation of marketing takes time. In a fee paying business, where the same people are the production resource and the promotional resource, how that time is made available, when and who does what, is crucial. Even in practices taking a real initiative with things marketing this often remains a problem, seemingly with no easy answers.

For those who tackle the process successfully, making real plans, laying responsibility, understanding and using the techniques appropriately – albeit with some experiment along

225

the way – there will be new business enquiries available. For those who pick up enquiries skilfully, in a truly sales orientated way, there will be new clients signed.

In a business where the feeling has traditionally been that 'nice guys don't sell' who can honestly say they do not get satisfaction from a client, or better still a new client, giving his final approval to a project? If you do not at present, or have not thought of it in that way, try it. There are more and more people in the profession who do, and more and more firms working hard to make sure it is a feeling that occurs to them more often.

For those who do all this and not only then turn in first class work, but manage and develop their clients purposefully, there are real opportunities for the future.

And opportunities, as was said in the preface, so often come disguised – as hard work. That alone is no doubt sufficient to ensure not everyone will succeed, but a marketing approach can make all the difference. The trick is to make it work for you.

Appendix·Revised guidelines on publicity and advertising

Issued by the Institute of Chartered Accountants in England and Wales and effective from 1 October 1984.

Statement 3. Publicity for and advertising of professional services

General

1. A member preparing or authorising the issue of material falling within this Statement should do so with a due sense of responsibility to the profession and to the public as a whole. In particular, such material should be in good taste both as to content and presentation and should not belittle services offered by others, whether members or not, either by claiming superiority for the services of a particular member or otherwise. The same attitude should be adopted towards activities mentioned in subsequent paragraphs.

2. Additionally, members who advertise should have in mind the requirements of the Advertising Standards Authority as to legality, decency, honesty and truthfulness.

3. Members should always have regard to the requirements of Statement 7.

Publicity

4. Publicity for members is acceptable.

Advertising

5. A member may advertise his services to the public.

6. To safeguard new entrants to the market and the competitive position of all firms regardless of their financial resources, advertisements should in size and scale be related to a requirement to inform rather than to impress. In pursuance of this principle advertisements in all newspapers should not exceed a quarter of a page; nor should advertisements by associated firms appearing in the same edition of a newspaper exceed in total that limit. Whilst specific limitations are not prescribed for advertisements appearing in media other than newspapers, similar restraint should be observed.

7. Advertisements may refer to the basis on which fees are calculated; however, the inclusion in an advertisement of hourly or other charging rates could be misleading and is not permissible.

8. A member may also advertise:
   (a) for staff, a partnership, salaried employment or for subcontract work;
   (b) on behalf of a client;
   (c) in a fiduciary or other capacity;
   (d) members' appointments, the opening of a new office, changes in the membership of a firm and changes in the name, address or telephone number of a firm.

Directories

9. A member may be listed in any directory whether printed or available through some other medium of communication.

Literature

10. Professional literature written or published by members, whether technical or descriptive of the services provided by the member, may be provided free to clients and to those who ask for it. It should not, however, be sent unsolicited to non-clients.

Sponsorship

11. A member's contribution to good causes, whether by way of donation or sponsorship, may be suitably and publicly acknowledged by the recipient. Appropriate causes for support include registered charities, education, sport and the arts. Members in doubt as to whether a prospective recipient falls within the above categories or wishing to venture outside them should, in good time, consult with the Ethics Committee.

Exhibitions and seminars

12. A member may participate in exhibitions, seminars and similar activities.

Explanatory notes on Statement 3

Good taste

1. Publicity and advertising material prepared or authorised by members must be consistent with the dignity of a profession.

2. Judgement as to what may or may not constitute good taste can only be made in the context of the particular facts on which that judgement is exercised. It is possible, however, to give some broad guidance and general examples as to what might, in appropriate circumstances, be regarded as not according with good taste. Thus material which tends to sensationalise or shock, or which is likely to give offence to religious beliefs, or is racist, is unacceptable. Other possible examples include the trivialisation of important issues, excessive reliance on a particular personality or personalities, the deriding of public figures, the disparagement of educational attainment and material which makes odious comparisons or is strident in tone, hectoring or extravagant.

Literature

3. Technical literature written or published by members of the Institute may be provided, unsolicited, to educational establishments, public libraries and other professional bodies. It may also be sent for review in publications with an interest in the subject matter of its content.

Statement 7

Obtaining professional work

1. A member should not in any circumstance obtain or seek professional work for himself or another member in an unprofessional manner.

2. In particular, a member should not obtain or seek professional work by direct mailing or by the practice commonly referred to as 'cold calling'.

3. A practising member should not give any commission, fee or reward to a third party, not being either his employee or another public accountant, in return for the introduction of a client.

4. A member who is an employee, other than an employee of a public accountant, should not, on behalf of his employer, carry on in his own name or in partnership any business which is normally carried on by a public accountant.

Explanatory notes on Statement 7

Cold calling

1. Cold calling is the act of making or instigating an unsolicited approach to a non-client with a view to obtaining professional work. It includes the act of making an appointment to call or making overtures by telephone or by letter.

Direct mailing

2. Subject to what is said in paragraph 3 below, direct mailing and the sending of unsolicited circulars, brochures or other literature about the firm to non-clients of the firm are forms of cold calling.

Contact with others

3. A member may inform others engaged in the provision of financial services to the public in the same locality of the services he himself can offer.

4. A member may invite holders of public office, as well as others engaged in the provision of financial services to the public, to attend specific events of relevance and importance to the community they serve.

Work for other organisations

5. There are many cases in which members in practice are retained by organisations which, in their turn, offer advice to their members on accountancy matters. The member retained by the organisation may, in relation to matters referred to him by the organisation, deal only with the organisation itself and not directly with any of its members. The member should ensure that any literature issued by the organisation in which his name or the name of his firm is mentioned conforms to the guidelines contained in Statement 3.